DAILY
WORD
for
FAMILIES

LINKING MY HEART
WITH THOSE I LOVE

Written and edited by Colleen Zuck,
Janie Wright, and Elaine Meyer

DAYBREAK

Daybreak Books
An Imprint of Rodale Books
Emmaus, Pennsylvania

Daybreak is a registered trademark of Rodale Press, Inc.

Printed in the United States of America on acid-free ∞,
recycled paper ♻

Cover Designer: Kristen Morgan Downey
Cover and Interior Illustrator: Vicki Wehrman

Library of Congress Cataloging-in-Publication Data

Zuck, Colleen.
    Daily word for families : linking my heart with those I love /
written and edited by Colleen Zuck, Janie Wright, and Elaine
Meyer.
      p.   cm.
   ISBN 1–57954–013–9 hardcover
   1. Family—Prayer-books and devotions—English.
2. Devotional calendars.   I. Wright, Janie.   II. Meyer, Elaine.
III. Title.
BV255.Z83   1999
249—dc21   99–37750

Distributed to the book trade by St. Martin's Press

2 4 6 8 10 9 7 5 3 1 hardcover

OUR PURPOSE

*"We publish books that empower
people's minds and spirits."*

An Invitation

Daily Word is the magazine of Silent Unity, a worldwide prayer ministry now in its second century of service. Silent Unity believes that:

- ◆ *all people are sacred*
- ◆ *God is present in all situations*
- ◆ *everyone is worthy of love, peace, health, and prosperity*

Silent Unity prays with all who ask for prayer. Every prayer request is held in absolute confidence, and there is never a charge. You are invited to contact Silent Unity 24 hours a day, any day of the year.

Write: Silent Unity, 1901 NW Blue Parkway
Unity Village, MO 64065-0001
Or call: (816) 969-2000   Fax: (816) 251-3554
Online: www.silentunity.org

There's More!

If you enjoy these inspirational messages, you may wish to subscribe to *Daily Word* magazine and receive a fresh, contemporary, uplifting message for each day of the month. With its inclusive, universal language, this pocket-size magazine is a friend to millions of people around the world.

For a free sample copy or for subscription information regarding *Daily Word* in English (regular and large-type editions) or in Spanish, please write:

Silent Unity, 1901 NW Blue Parkway
Unity Village, MO 64065-0001
Or call: (800) 669-0282   Fax: (816) 251-3554
Online: www.dailyword.org

List of Articles

INTRODUCTION

L ike most people, you are probably searching for ways to enrich your relationships with family and friends. The good news is that there is a way: Think positive, loving thoughts about others and envision positive, loving interactions with them. Thoughts have tremendous formative power. They shape every word that is spoken and every action that is taken.

Relax for a moment and allow yourself to experience the power of your thoughts. Leaving behind all judgments about people and situations from the past, envision yourself in a sacred circle in which love, commitment, and acceptance flow between you and another person in your family or among all members of your family. Feel that love and let it begin to soothe your heart and mind. Oh, how good it feels to be loving and loved!

The meditations, prayers, and articles in this book will help the sacred quality of love become a reality in your life—whether you are longing for more love in your long-term relationships or those that are newly formed.

Daily Word for Families is a daily source of help and inspiration for individuals within a family and for the family as a whole. Our hope is that the ideas presented here will resonate within the soul and quicken an awareness of the spirit of God within all people.

No one is left out. From seniors to children old enough to read or be read to, each person will discover ideas and principles for enriching the soul and enriching relationships.

As you read and pray every day, continue to create a

picture of a circle of loving people in your mind. Look around the circle. See the smiling faces. Do you recognize it as the family you are now? If so, good. If not, then recognize that you are envisioning the family you desire, the family that you are helping become a reality thought by thought, prayer by prayer each day.

Such a vision can be a reality, because whatever you can perceive and believe in, individually or collectively with others, can be achieved. Within you is the wisdom and power of the Almighty. You *can* be the loving person in a loving family that God created you to be!

How to Use This Book

1. **Articles:** Throughout the book, you will find a rich source of inspiration in the true-life experiences of actress June Allyson, "The Family Circus" creator and cartoonist Bil Keane, TV game show host Bob Barker, singer Naomi Judd, and others. The tremendous overcoming and spiritual insight shared in these stories are not only interesting reading but also reminders of what God can accomplish through willing hearts.

2. **Daily messages:** Each meditation is written in the voice of the individual. Reserve 10 to 30 minutes a day for reading a meditation and spending time in prayer. Reading aloud softly may help you to imprint the message more clearly in your mind so that you will make it a part of your daily living.

As you read the life-enriching quotes of people from all walks of life, you will identify with your own humanness. Reading the Bible verses will open you to a greater awareness of your own sacredness and the sacredness of the special people who share your home, your life, and your heart. The practical applications presented in the text offer you ideas for thinking and acting and living from the love of God within you.

3. **For the Children:** Interspersed throughout the daily messages are tender prayers especially for children. Although these meditations are written for children at third-grade and higher reading levels, even younger children will be captivated by the pictures created in their minds as the prayers are read to them. Themes of recognizing the presence of God, being courageous in the dark, and emerging spiritual awareness are presented as the voice of a child talking to God.

4. **Circle of Love:** Circle-of-Love pages are written as the voice of unity within the family. These meditations unite couples and generations within the family in a circle of love. The experience of unity is a commitment of love and harmony that infuses relationships with understanding, peace, and compassion.

While you are reading *Daily Word for Families*, you will discover what readers of *Daily Word* magazine have said again and again: "*Daily Word* is written especially for me."

As you allow yourself to fully *experience* the stories, quotes, Bible verses, and meditations, you will also inscribe them on your heart and soul so that they will bless you and your family all the days of your lives.

—The Editors

Angels at My Side
by June Allyson

My father left home when I was six years old, so my mother and I moved in with my grandmother, who became the center of my life for the next few years. She was my guardian angel. When she died, my security was gone, or so I thought.

Less than a year later, life got even harder. A severe storm roared through the New York area with high winds and heavy rains. When it passed, I grabbed my bike and headed out to see what havoc the storm had created. As I passed beneath a big, old, decaying tree, I heard a sickening crack. I turned just in time to see the tree coming straight at me. The falling tree hit me squarely, breaking half the bones in my body.

My mother and I were already living in abject poverty, and now it was questionable if I would even survive with such massive injuries. God had a plan, however, which included Earthly angels already in place to help me. My doctor had a wonderful, loving manner and inspired me to want to live. The nurses hovered over my small body, helping me to find comfortable positions.

Even though the doctor and the nurses were cheering my every move, no one believed that I would ever walk again.

A swimming instructor, Marie Spinosa, heard about my injuries and volunteered her entire summer to my recovery. "What is lost can be recovered," Miss Spinosa would tell me daily as she guided me around in the pool, slowly rebuilding my atrophied muscles and limbering up my reluctant limbs. On days that I felt well enough to venture out, some of my friends from school would push my wheelchair to the local movie house, and I would sit for hours watching Ginger Rogers and Fred Astaire pictures. As I sat in the darkened theater, another dream began to fill my heart.

I promised God that if I were able to walk again, I would not only walk, I would dance. I would earn enough as an entertainer to get my mother and me out of poverty and, hopefully, bring happiness to others.

Because of Miss Spinosa's unrelenting guidance, I began to recover. Soon I was out of the wheelchair and on crutches. Finally, I advanced to using a brace. I worked up enough courage to experiment with dancing—haltingly at first, because I was hampered by the brace.

Once I was back in school, I told my girlfriends that I could dance as well as Ginger and Fred. Skeptics one and all, they showed me a newspaper notice announcing auditions for a new Broadway musical. When one of my friends bet me a quarter that I was too scared to go, I said, "What's the address?"

When the piano player asked for my music, I said,

"What music?" I finally came up with the name of a popular tune of the day. Miraculously, I was asked to return the following day. At the callback, I was in the middle of the same song, actually in mid-word, when a voice cut in from the dark in front of the stage: "No, no, hold it!" The man continued, "Please, please, we've got to hire her—if we don't, she'll come back and sing that song again and again, and I can't stand it!" There was a huge laugh at the end of his little speech. The voice belonged to Richard Rogers, who had written the song! So I got the job, won the quarter, and found a way to keep my promise to God.

Throughout my life—during my career at MGM; my wonderful marriage to actor Dick Powell, which included our precious children, Pam and Richard; my blessed marriage to Dr. David Ashrow after Dick's death; and my favorite role as grandmother to grandson Rickie—the spirit of God has been with me. God has guided my life and career with a loving hand and continued to send angels when I needed them most.

What my husband Dick said to me many times is true: "Junie, God is love." Yes, Dick, you were so very right. God is love, and I thank God for filling my life with loving people who have been angels at my side.

Day 1

——◆——

*Thought by thought, you can change your outlook
and your attitude. Thought by thought, you
can change your life.—Martha Smock*

**ENRICHING
MY
FAMILY**

When more love, understanding, and harmony are needed in a family, it's really a change of heart by the individuals that is needed. I pray for a change—not to change the other people in my family, but for the wisdom to realize that the only person I am responsible for changing or am able to change is me.

I can be the one to bring more love, understanding, and harmony into my family. I can do this through my thoughts, my words, and my actions. I prepare myself through my daily times of prayer and meditation.

When I pray, I feel my vital connection with God's spirit within me. I am peaceful, and I contribute peace to my relationships. Then something magical happens: The more loving and peaceful I am, the more I encourage the members of my family to express these qualities.

**I bring love, understanding, and harmony
to my relationships with my family.**

Day 2

—◆—

The greatest power in the world, the power of God,
is aptly described by the phrase "power to give."
—Ernest C. Wilson

CAREGIVER It seems incredible, but when my whole purpose in doing something is to bless someone else, I also receive a blessing. Because of my deep desire to enrich the lives of others, my life is enriched.

I have reverence and appreciation for all the gracious, loving people who are caregivers. I know that it takes special people to make a commitment to be a friend and helper to others. I also know that because God lives in every person, we are all capable of being caregivers.

I give thanks to all who answer the call to give of themselves in caring for others. And I give thanks that God is the source of the unlimited love, understanding, and wisdom that they give.

God is the source of all that I need to be
a loving, generous caregiver.

Day 3

—◆—

*Family rituals are
the cornerstone of closeness.
—David Elkind*

**ONE
IN
SPIRIT**

Whatever role I fill in my home or school, or whatever position I occupy in my workplace, I am united with others by this truth: We are filled with the spirit of God, and we live in the presence of God.

I may not know why I am where I am in my life experiences or where I will go in helping to complete a divine plan, but I do know that the same God that created the earth I am standing on and the air I am breathing also created me.

The Gospel of John (3:8) explains: "The wind blows where it chooses, and you hear the sound of it, but you do not know where it comes from or where it goes. So it is with everyone who is born of the Spirit."

Knowing why I am here is not what is most important. What is important is what I learn and how I grow throughout my life.

**I am one in spirit with God and one in spirit
with my family and friends.**

Day 4

—◆—

There is no separation in love. We are always one
with God and one with those we love.
—May Rowland

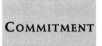

COMMITMENT

Couples find inspiration in the renewing of their wedding vows, individuals discover new creativity in renewing a commitment to a cause, and whole neighborhoods of people come together as one in a commitment to community.

Loving words, thoughtful actions, and feelings of unity are stirred up by a renewal of my commitment to a relationship or a purpose. Yet one of the greatest renewals I can experience is through a commitment to God—as I make or renew a commitment to bring an awareness of God into my marriage, my family, my friendships, my community, or my work.

So whether I am making a new commitment or renewing a long-standing one, this day can be a time of renewal for me. It will be when I dedicate myself to God and my life to expressing the spirit of God.

This is a day of renewal!

Day 5
—◆—

*Spiritual love means compassionate involvement
where there is a need to be met.*
—William L. Fischer

LOVE

God loves me, and because I am a member of God's universal family, love is my divine heritage. I feel great joy in sharing that love with all people.

My heart's desire is to be a light of love to the world. Being a light of love is an honor, and I act accordingly. Like all humankind, I have been chosen to play a role in the lives of others, and I joyfully fulfill my divine purpose by being a living, breathing expression of God's love. In all my relationships, I express love and understanding.

I extend love to all God's creations. When I am out in and exploring the world of nature, I act responsibly and lovingly toward all God's creatures. I love all that God has created.

I am a light of love in the world.

Day 6

—◆—

What feeling is so nice as a child's hand in yours?
So small, so soft and warm, like a kitten huddling
in the shelter of your clasp.—Marjorie Holmes

**B E
G E N T L E**

During stressful times, I can be the most critical of myself, and this just intensifies the level of stress I am already experiencing.

What I need to remember is to be gentle with myself and to be gentle with others. A gentle attitude, a gentle voice, and gentle actions penetrate to the core of me and others, absorbing anger in much the same way that a sponge absorbs spilled water.

Gentleness acts as an impenetrable filter that shields me from the harshness of others and keeps me from reacting emotionally. Out of gentleness, I can and do respond through the inspiration of Spirit. And it is that gentle inspiration that revives my awareness of my spiritual nature—even in the middle of a crisis.

God inspires me to be gentle with myself and others.

Day 7

—◆—

How very good and pleasant it is
when kindred live together in unity.
—Psalms 133:1

Just as each drop in the ocean is a part of the greater whole, each person on Earth is an important part of God's family, a vital link in a connection with one another.

And just as each drop of the ocean contains all the elements that make up the whole ocean, each person has within that spark of divinity—God's loving spirit— which unites everyone.

God lives in me and in every person on Earth! God's spirit within is what connects everyone in a unity of purpose and creates a sacred union that links the people of the world together in love.

I am united in mind, heart, and spirit with God and with others. Through this divine connection, I can never be alone. I am never without the love and support I need.

God's spirit connects us all in a sacred union of love.

Day 8

—◆—

*If people daily practiced forgiveness, they would probably
put most doctors . . . social workers, and loan companies
out of business, because everyone would become healthy
and prosperous.—Catherine Ponder*

FORGIVE

One of the greatest actions I can
take in building peaceful feelings
within myself and harmony with
others is to forgive—fully and
completely. More than anything else, forgiveness is an
attitude of heart and spirit that, when expressed freely,
will grow stronger.

Yet before I truly begin to forgive others, I first learn
to forgive myself. Any mistakes I made in the past are
over and done with now. I am a work in progress, so I
have something to learn from each day's experiences.
Because I have broken free of any negativity from the
past, I am capable of forgiving myself and others.

Yesterday has come and gone, and the time to forgive
is now.

**I can and do forgive myself and others—
fully and completely.**

Day 9

---◆---

*The roads we take are more important than
the goals we announce. Decisions determine destiny.*
—Frederick Speakman

**DIVINE
ORDER**

What do I do when I am facing a
momentous decision—one that can no
longer be postponed? And what can I
do to help someone I care about who
is going through something that will dramatically
change his life?

I take heart and know that times such as these can be
easier and less stressful when I remember that divine
order is already active in my life and in the lives of my
loved ones.

In prayer and meditation, I ask God for understanding
so that I will know that the decisions I make and the
actions I take are in line with divine order.

I have reached this point in my life with the help of
God, so I know that the rest of my journey will be in
the companionship of God and to the accompaniment
of divine order.

**Trusting in God and the order of God,
I make wise decisions.**

Day 10

—◆—

I never lose an opportunity of urging a practical beginning, however small, for it is wonderful how often the mustard seed germinates and roots itself.—Florence Nightingale

NEW BEGINNINGS The maintenance and repair on most cars call for a financial investment, but such an investment in my car ensures that my family and I will have dependable transportation.

So it is in life. I invest in my own well-being by taking care of myself and making needed adjustments in my life, including new beginnings. An awareness of God in me and in my life is an investment in spiritual understanding.

Moving from one place to another, making a commitment to a relationship or moving past one, beginning a career or changing one, I may feel as if I am starting over. And I can—with God as my guide. Every moment I am becoming more aware of God, so every moment is a great new beginning.

This day is a great new beginning for me.

Day 11

—◆—

*The cornerstone of peace is love, and love is
the assignment of this generation, the fulfillment
of the "new heaven and the new earth" wherein
all humanity is unified.—Sue Sikking*

**INNER
PEACE**

Knowing that the love of God is embracing me at all times brings serenity to my soul. As I quietly affirm *God loves me,* I feel peace resonating within me. I glow with inner peace.

God loves me. I actively live my life knowing that the peace of God helps cushion any bumps I may experience along my journey.

God loves me. I am a beloved member of a divinely created world, and I am cared for by my Creator, the One Power in all the universe.

God loves me. As I bask in the glow of unconditional love, I am confident. Knowing I can never be separated from God's greatness, I am at peace.

**I feel the inner peace of a spiritual being,
for this is who I am.**

Day 12

—◆—

I think this is what hooks one on gardening:
It is the closest one can come to being
present at the creation.
—Phyllis Theroux

A SACRED WORK

When winter disappears and evidence of spring bursts forth everywhere, I marvel at the order of nature. The rich, green grass provides a glorious background for newly budding flowers, and abundant foliage provides cover for birds and other creatures.

Still, I may wonder about the order of my own life—especially if things seem a bit chaotic. Yet I know there is a sacred order at work. I find reassurance in Jesus' words: "Consider the lilies of the field . . . they neither toil nor spin, yet I tell you, even Solomon in all his glory was not clothed like one of these." (Matthew 6:28–29)

Yes, there is a sacred order at work in my life. So I look to the presence of God instead of appearances, and I understand that God is clothing me in the glory of love and joy.

I rejoice, for there is a sacred order at work everywhere in God's universe.

Day 13
———◆———

You have to leave the city of your comfort and go into the wilderness of your intuition. What you'll discover will be wonderful. What you'll discover will be yourself.
—Alan Alda

CELEBRATE LIFE

Planning a vacation or a trip can sometimes be as fun and fulfilling as the actual event. Yet even before I study the maps or pack my bags, there is something more important that I can do.

I pray—not necessarily to make the order of the world conform to me and my plans, but to get myself spiritually centered so that whatever I do, I am consciously aware of God.

Then my life is a celebration—whether I am on vacation or at work or school, in my own home or far away. In fact, I feel at home and at peace wherever I travel.

I find such joy in celebrating the life God has created me to live! I marvel at and enjoy the world of wonder God has created!

I live each day as a celebration of the life God has created me to live.

Day 14

—◆—

I am careful not to confuse excellence with perfection.
Excellence, I can reach for; perfection is God's business.
—Michael J. Fox

GRACE

How great it would be to play a game that I could not possibly lose or to take a test that I could not fail! Yet, because the grace of God has been given to me, I can be sure that I am never a failure—even if I feel I have failed. Each experience, whether completely successful or not, is a chance for me to learn and grow.

I am a joyful receiver of God's grace, accepting the pure, unconditional love that I have been so freely given. Divine love nurtures and blesses me.

As I gain greater and greater spiritual understanding, I embrace the splendor of God's grace in action around me.

With peace and love in my heart, I gratefully say, "Thank You, God!"

I am nurtured and blessed by the grace of God.

Day 15

—◆—

If you limit your choices only to what seems possible or reasonable, you disconnect yourself from what you truly want, and all that is left is a compromise.—Robert Fritz

CHOICES

When I am working on a project that doesn't seem to be going well, I may begin to doubt my ability to get it done right or on time. Or I can choose to believe that God will help me get the job done. I choose God.

If people in my life are acting in ways that upset me, I may become angry and judgmental based on how I feel they should act. Or I can choose to rely on God to show me how to be loving, compassionate, and accepting. I choose God.

There will always be events that I am not able to control. In every situation, however, it is up to me to decide how I will respond. I can become caught up in the situation, or I can choose to let God lift my thoughts above the situation to the solution. I choose God.

God is the highest and best choice I can make.

Day 16

For the Children

Hello God,

Grownups have told me not to be afraid, even when I am by myself, because You are with me. They say, "You may not see God, but when you are quiet and thinking of God, you will know that God is with you."

So, God, I am wondering if You touched my face first thing this morning when I was quiet and still in bed? Just before I opened my eyes, I felt the softest of touches. At first, I thought maybe it was just a friendly breeze blowing in my window, but then I wondered if You were saying good morning.

I felt happy just thinking that You were waking me up. I didn't mind eating breakfast or getting ready for school. So thanks, God, for saying, "Good morning. Time to get up!" You said it in a way that made me feel good.

And, God, I have one more question: Did You hear me when I said "Good morning" to You?

Day 17

—◆—

*Thanksgiving is a vital part of our nature; it is
as necessary in our lives as rain is to the thirsty soil.*
—*Vera Dawson Tait*

APPRECIATE GOD

God, I appreciate You. Letting that appreciation speak through my prayers, my words, and my actions sets off a virtual reverberation of gladness within me.

God, I appreciate life. I am thankful that Your spirit is within me and breathes through me. Life is precious!

God, I appreciate others. I have such sweet memories of those who have touched my life, who have taught me and nurtured me. I am in awe of the diversity of Your love as it is expressed through people everywhere.

God, I appreciate my home. It is more than just the place where I eat and sleep and find shelter. I give thanks for the beauty and wonder of planet Earth—for sunshine and rain, for fresh air and clear streams, for mountaintops and the depths of the ocean.

**I appreciate God and the wonder of God
that is everywhere!**

Day 18

—◆—

The lesson which life repeats and constantly enforces is
"look underfoot." You are always nearer the divine and
the true source of your power than you think.
—John Burroughs

DIVINE
ATMOSPHERE

The incredibly complex way the tiniest creature comes to life is miraculous—a reminder that God, who breathed the miracle of life into me, will also take care of me.

I just naturally flourish in an atmosphere of love, and this is the atmosphere that God has created and is continuing to create around me, around the world, and around the universe. So wherever I am and wherever I go, I live and thrive in a divine atmosphere.

I know this truth for my loved ones also. When I pray for them and even think of them, I envision them in an atmosphere of divine love and life. No matter how far away they may be, I know that the spirit of God has given them life and also refreshes and directs their lives.

My loved ones and I flourish in an atmosphere
of love and life that God has created.

DAILY WORD FOR FAMILIES

Day 19

—◆—

Some people are still unaware that reality contains unparalleled beauties. The fantastic and unexpected, the ever-changing and renewing is nowhere so exemplified as in real life itself.—Bernice Abbott

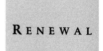

RENEWAL

This is a turning point for me—a resurrection of the soul, a renewal of life, activities, and purpose. I turn from thinking about faults and limitations to knowing that God lives within me, within my loved ones, and within every person in the world.

People the world over are going through a resurrection experience of the soul. Person by person, the whole world is being renewed by an understanding of our universal oneness.

I give thanks for God's spirit of life within me, and I add the light of my spiritual awareness to the light of spiritual awareness of the individuals around me. Oh, how brightly divine light shines! We are renewed in realizing that we are one family sharing a home in a universe of God's creation.

> **Through God's spirit of life within me,
> I am renewed.**

Day 20

—◆—

Laughter is a form of internal jogging. It moves your internal organs around. It enhances respiration. It is an igniter of great expectations.—Norman Cousins

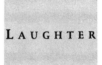

LAUGHTER

How loving of God to give me not only an endless, internal source of joy but also to provide me with laughter as a way of expressing that joy.

Laughter is a key that unlocks joy within me and sends a current of energy rushing through me. It is amazing that when I feel my energy level is at its lowest, a hearty laugh is an instant boost to my stamina. Gladness rises from within me and relaxes my muscles all along the way, relieving any tension.

Laughter is the joy of Spirit tickling my soul and the energy of Spirit healing my body.

As I laugh, the spirit of God flows through me in a rush of gladness.

Day 21

——◆——

*Climb the mountains and get their good tidings.
Nature's peace will flow into you as sunshine flows
into trees. The winds will blow their own freshness
into you . . . while cares will drop away from you
like the leaves of Autumn.—John Muir*

**GOD'S
BEAUTY**

I appreciate the beauty that God
has created—the people I love, the
majesty of nature. I appreciate all that
humankind has invented and built
as God's instruments. Most important of all, I
appreciate God.

God's spirit permeates everything that exists, all that I
know and feel and believe. God exists in my thoughts
and in the very energy it takes to think these thoughts.
Understanding that God is everywhere and in
everything, I know that God is the source of all I will
ever need or desire.

As I recognize the presence of God, I acknowledge
the one true source of all beauty. And it is in knowing
God that I am truly blessed.

I appreciate God's beauty everywhere.

Day 22

— ◆ —

I do not pray for success;
I ask for faithfulness.
—Mother Teresa

FAITH God, in times of both joy and challenge, You are there for me. I have faith in You, for You have seen me through all the ups and downs of life. I give thanks to You for guiding me each day.

Thank You, God, for the peace of mind I receive from Your loving presence. I have faith that Your love will always sustain me.

Thank You, God, for the people in my life. I always want to be a blessing to them because they are such a blessing to me.

Thank You, God, for providing me with clean air to breathe and nourishing food to eat. I share Earth with all life, and I am fortunate to be one of Your creations.

God, the greatest "Thank You" I can give is my eternal love and faith in You, and I joyously do so today and every day.

My faith is in God, the creator and sustainer of all life.

Day 23

—◆—

Many a humble soul will be amazed to find that the
seed it sowed in weakness, in the dust of daily life, has
blossomed into immortal flowers under the eye of the Lord.
—*Harriet Beecher Stowe*

PATIENCE

After planting a seed, I patiently wait for the first sign of new growth. During this time of patience, however, I realize that the miracle of new life is taking shape.

The patience I give to that seed I also extend to myself and others. Everyone needs time to develop understanding and other skills. Being patient, I dedicate myself to living in this moment—not in the future—and trusting that God's order will prevail.

I understand that my blessings will come at the right time and in the right way. Knowing this, I can be patient with anyone I may encounter. And I find that a little patience goes a long way in promoting better relationships with everyone.

I am patient.

Day 24

— ◆ —

*Joy is the laughter of God. Joy is a habit and
a habitation of the heart that abides in God's love.*
—James Dillet Freeman

JOY

Spending time with a child can be a wonderful lesson in how to feel and express joy.

Children just naturally seem to express joy: They laugh and play with abandon, enjoying each moment as it comes. And they should, because joy is a natural part of living, a treasure from God that is meant to be shared.

Feeling joy and expressing joy are both within the divine plan. Without joy, how could I ever appreciate the wonder of creation or the beauty of the world in which I live? Without joy, how could I ever feel fulfilled by anything I do?

I am filled with joy because I am filled with the spirit of God. I give expression to the joy that is already within me! I honor God by feeling joyful and expressing joy to the world.

I am filled to overflowing with joy!

Day 25

—◆—

We all have the extraordinary coded within us,
waiting to be released.
—Jean Houston

LET GO,
LET GOD

I turn to God each day in prayer—whether I have a challenge or not. Yet certain situations require more time to be resolved, so I need an extra measure of strength—in mind and heart—that only God can give me.

As I release worries to the wisdom of God, I free myself to be a source of prayer support for everyone.

I can let go of worry when I consider how beautifully the universe and nature function in an intricate balance without my interference. Seeing the sheer magnitude of God's power and order, I find it easier to completely let go and let God be in charge.

There is an order—a divine plan—that is always present, so I rest in the realization that God is in charge.

Knowing that God is in charge, I let go
and let God bring about a divine plan.

Day 26

—◆—

Remember, there's no such thing as a small act
of kindness. Every act creates a ripple with no logical end.
—Scott Adams

REMEMBER Sweet memories of people can take
me to a sacred place. I remember the
ones who are near and dear to me,
those very special people who have
encouraged me when I needed it, supported me when
times were rough, and loved me just as I was and now
am. I give thanks that they shared my life.

Whether the people I remember are still with me or
have moved on, I am grateful for the influence they
have had on me and on the world.

Today can be a day for knowing that every person
on Earth is a member of God's universal family. I
remember to bless the people of all nations of the
world. As I think of the world family, I bless everyone
in my prayers and send out loving thoughts of peace
and goodwill.

I remember the family of God in my prayers.

Day 27

—◆—

God is love, and those who abide in love abide
in God, and God abides in them.
—1 John 4:16

**G O D
I S M Y
S E C U R I T Y**

Knowing the security of God's love and caring is a tremendous blessing to me as I go about my day.

With God's love embracing me, I have no fear of what could happen or what might happen. I do know beyond a doubt that the presence of God is always with me. My confidence is in God.

God is also with the people whom I love and care about, and I do not take their security or my own for granted. Instead, I give thanks for the peace of mind that comes from knowing we are safe and securely encompassed in God's presence and love, wherever we may be.

> God is my security, and I am at peace knowing
> that the presence of God is with me
> and my loved ones—always.

Day 28

—◆—

To pray for another
is healing to the self.
—Connie Fillmore Bazzy

PRAYER FOR OTHERS I may be right there in the same room with someone I care about and want to help but still may not be able to express how much I care, how much I want to be of help. Maybe this is because I don't know what to say or do.

However, I don't feel helpless because I know how I can be helpful. I can pray with and for this person, whether we are together or separated by many miles. The spirit of God within me and my loved one unites us at all times.

Prayer is a bridge of faith that links me, heart and soul, with all my loved ones. So each time I pray, I am tapping into a vital spiritual connection that inspires and encourages me and those for whom I am praying to be aware of God—God within us and God within our incredible world.

With prayer, I build a bridge of faith
that unites me with others.

Day 29

—◆—

Love is the completeness of life. If there has been
the omission of a kindness, love puts itself into the gap
and more than compensates for the deficiency.
—Imelda Shanklin

NURTURING LOVE

God, even before I took that first breath of life or felt my first human embrace, Your love was there waiting for me to experience it and to give expression to it. Your love for me and within me is a continual blessing.

I give thanks that divine love lives in me and that divine love lives through me as a desire to care about and for all that You have created. The more love I express, the more love I experience.

Love flowing from me joins with love expressed by others. In a unity of love, we nourish everyone and everything on Earth. In a spirit of love, we are always willing to be patient and kind, attentive and understanding, forgiving and hopeful of the best.

Thank You, God, for Your nurturing love and
for each person who is open to sharing Your love.

Day 30

———◆———

Circle of Love

What power there is in love to heal, to comfort, and to restore—power that transcends feelings and emotions. When we share pure unconditional love through our thoughts, words, and actions, we are declaring that we recognize one another as spiritual beings, and we are fulfilling a divine purpose.

Love—divine love—unites us as a family, as an individual family and as God's universal family. So let us, in prayer, bring our family into a circle of love. We leave no one out, because we recognize all people as members of God's universal family.

Love creates a sacred circle in which we join heart and soul with our spouses, children, parents, and friends. And the power of God moves from person to person to bless and to heal, to encourage and to inspire.

> *He drew a circle that shut me out—*
> *Heretic, rebel, a thing to flout.*
> *But Love and I had the wit to win:*
> *We drew a circle that took him in.*
> *—Edwin Markham*

THE SECRET INGREDIENT
BY BIL KEANE

I have heard that copies of my "The Family Circus" cartoons are posted on refrigerators everywhere. Frankly, I would rather have my work hanging on refrigerators, where it reaches many lives, than secluded in a museum where only a few can see it.

People often thank me for a particular feature that brings a touch of enlightenment to their day. They thank me profusely for injecting a bit of spirituality into the cartoon. But when I first started the cartoon 40 years ago, I was criticized for mentioning God or for having the children—in a playful way—mispronounce the Lord's Prayer. Jeffy would say, "Our Father, who art in heaven, how did you know my name?" Soon, however, people began to realize that the cartoon represented what was happening in real life—in their own families—and they loved it.

Being home full-time in 1959 with my wife, Thel, and our children—Gayle, Neal, Glen, Chris, and Jeff—gave me inspiration for a new cartoon series, "The Family Circus." It featured a mom, a dad, and three children—Billy, Dolly, and Jeffy. Several years later, PJ was added. The syndicate agreed to distribute "The Family Circus" and sold it to 19 newspapers in 1960. The cartoon has

*"If God lives inside us like Grandma says,
I hope He likes peanut butter and jelly."*

grown in popularity and is now featured in more than 1,500 newspapers. Readership is estimated to be around 100 million people daily.

Later on, the characters of the grandfather and grandmother were introduced. In one cartoon, Granddad, who was a spirit in Heaven, was sitting on a cloud enjoying watching his grandchildren down on Earth. People wrote to say, "Thank you, thank you, for giving us a way to show our children where their grandfather has gone." The comic pages may have seemed an unlikely place for a portrayal of eternal life, but it was a graphic depiction that comforted both children and adults.

People relate to the spiritual insight of the "The Family Circus" children when they describe Heaven as a great big hug that lasts forever or explain that the snow-covered landscape is God's way of putting a topping on everything.

People also relate to "Mommy"—modeled after my wife, Thel—who was and is the backbone of our family. Thel has such a great grasp on family life and what it means to raise children in a loving, happy environment. I try to illustrate this philosophy in the cartoons, and I receive a lot of credit for it, but Thel is the real inspiration and heart of "The Family Circus."

Our five children are all grown now and have careers and families of their own. We have nine grandchildren, and I follow them around just waiting for them to do something funny or cute! The things our children did growing up seem even funnier now, so I incorporate a good bit of nostalgia into my cartoons, especially on the Sunday pages. I like to remind people of the joy of having children around the house, to encourage parents to enjoy their children at every age and every stage.

Since I began "The Family Circus," the world and the family structure have changed dramatically. But the

". . . Andy walks with me . . .
Andy talks with me . . . "

family unit is still important—no matter what the makeup of the family may be. I think this is the secret ingredient in "The Family Circus": the realization that a family setting in which the parents love their children and, in turn, the children love their parents is the happiest place in the world to be.

Day 31

— ◆ —

*To achieve the impossible, it is precisely
the unthinkable that must be thought.*
—Tom Robbins

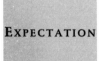

EXPECTATION There may be times when I feel upset or disappointed because others have fallen short of my expectations. I may then feel as if I have lost faith in them.

But I can avoid such heartache when I realize that people can only live up to their own expectations. This is true for me also. I love my friends and family, but it is in God that I place my faith.

My faith is in God, so I expect the best! I know without a doubt that God loves me, and I do not doubt that God will always be there for me. No matter where I go or what I am doing, God is with me to help and encourage me, to love and inspire me, to guide and protect me.

My unwavering faith in God assures me that divine order is always at work in my life and in the lives of the ones I love.

My faith is in God, so I expect the best!

Day 32

— ◆ —

When we do the best that we can, we never know what
miracle is wrought in our life, or in the life of another.
—Helen Keller

THROUGH IT ALL

Dear God, how can I find words that explain how much love and appreciation I feel for all that You have done for me? I cannot, so I let my faith and my actions speak for me. In all that I do, I dedicate myself to living from Your love and wisdom.

Through my kind and compassionate words to others, Your message of hope and inspiration is on my lips, and Your love for all humankind is in my heart.

My actions reflect the creative spirit that You have instilled within me. I help others whenever it is possible to do so, and I use my time and talents to the betterment of all.

Through my quiet times of prayer, I bless my family and friends with prayers of love and thanksgiving. We are beautiful expressions of Your love and instruments of Your peace.

I dedicate myself to letting the spirit of God
be reflected in all that I do.

Day 33

———◆———

The purpose of life is the
expansion of happiness.
—Maharishi Mahesh Yogi

ENTHUSIASM

Laughing with friends and loved ones is one of the pure joys of life. Laughter dissolves tension, warms the heart, and brightens the day.

The joy I express through fun and laughter flows out from the spirit of God within me as an enthusiasm that is to be enjoyed, shared, and remembered fondly. And it is only natural that I want to share these feelings with others, spreading joy and goodwill to those I meet throughout the day.

The joy of God is in my heart. I give thanks for life—for the joy in life—and for the love and companionship of family and friends. I cannot help but greet this day with joy and enthusiasm, for I am filled with the life and vitality of God!

I greet this day with joy and enthusiasm!

Day 34

—◆—

Trust yourself. You know more
than you think you do.
—Benjamin Spock

POSITIVE INFLUENCE God, I give thanks for all the people who have been a positive influence in my life, and I am grateful for Your guidance in helping me to be a positive influence for others.

Through Your love and inspiration, You show me the treasure I have in friends and family, in my home and work, in the miracle of my very existence. Your wisdom is a bright light along the way, and I pray that I will be a beacon of Your light for others.

With unconditional love and acceptance, I always look for the best in everyone. I know that the people in my life are here for a reason, and I want to be the blessing for them that they are for me.

God, thank You for helping me to love others and
to be a positive influence in their lives.

Day 35

—◆—

Life is a series of experiences, each one of which makes us bigger. . . . We must learn that the setbacks and griefs which we endure help us in our marching onward.
—*Henry Ford*

DIVINE SANCTUARY

With headlines and reports heralding the negative news of the world, it is only natural that I think about ways to protect my loved ones—even wanting to build a protective shelter around them.

However, because God is always with us, I do not have to hide myself or my loved ones from the world. The power that causes the sun to rise and set, that provides all things necessary to sustain life, and that created me and my loved ones, is the same power that protects and nurtures each one of us.

I can retreat at any time to a divine sanctuary by turning to God in prayer and meditation. In silence, God waits for me, ready to reassure me that I am loved and protected.

God is a sanctuary of love and peace for me and my loved ones.

Day 36

—◆—

The greatest sin—perhaps the only sin—
passion can commit is to be joyless.
—*Dorothy L. Sayers*

REKINDLE THE SPIRIT
Concentrating on all the responsibilities I have—maintaining a home, raising children, and meeting schedules—I sometimes forget to honor the sacred spirit within me. Yet I can rekindle that spirit in any moment by keeping my thoughts in touch with God.

And my reward is great: love and joy, happiness and peace, hope and faith—which are available to me at all times. In prayer to God, I really know in my heart that I am a glorious expression of the spirit of God within me!

The spirit of God is alive and well in my heart and in my soul. This spirit reawakens in me an awareness of the joy of knowing God in every moment of my life. My every expectation is fulfilled, and I enjoy a celebration of love and faith every day of the year.

In touch with God, I am spiritually refreshed.

Day 37

——◆——

We are all cells in the same
body of humanity.
—Peace Pilgrim

UNIVERSAL ONENESS

When I look at a block of stone, what do I see? A sculptor might see a future piece of art. A builder might see a piece that would fit beautifully in a stone wall or walkway. A child would surely see a stepping-stone for reaching new heights.

Are any of these visions wrong? Of course not. They are simply different possibilities from different points of view. But the stone is the same regardless of who is looking at it.

My own view of the Creator may be different from the views of others. Varying names for the One Power have sprung up in many different cultures—God, Spirit, Yahweh, Allah—yet the divine Presence is the same.

We are all created by the same Master Creator, destined to fulfill our own divine potential. We are one people, one mind, one voice of peace and love.

We are one in spirit.

Day 38

—◆—

It is good to have an end to journey toward;
but it is the journey that matters, in the end.
—Ursula K. Le Guin

No Other Way

If I have reached a point in my life where I cannot seem to make sense of what is happening to me or around me, I can put things in perspective by remembering these inspiring words by Martha Smock:

Could we but see the pattern of our days . . .
By which we came to this, the present time,
This place in life; we should see the climb
Our soul has made up through the years.
We should forget the hurts, the wanderings,
    the fears . . .
And know that we could come no other way.

These words bring a real sense of the order that is present in my life. Through grace, I am assured that there is a reason and a purpose for what is happening in my life. I know that each experience is leading my soul to the mountaintop.

Every day of my life has reason and purpose.

Day 39

—◆—

Patience with others is Love,
Patience with self is Hope,
Patience with God is Faith.
—Adel Bestavros

GOLDEN THREAD
Jesus shared life-enriching spiritual principles that were woven like golden threads throughout the tapestry of His stories. When the apostles asked how they could have more faith, Jesus explained the incredible power in just a little faith—the size of a mustard seed. (Luke 17:5–6)

So if I am facing a challenge and feel as though I need great faith, I remember what a little faith can do. My faith does not make God more powerful, for God is all power. But it does remind me to release the power of God that is always within me—waiting to heal and comfort me as well as help me prosper.

The possibilities are unlimited. And like the golden threads in a tapestry, my faith is a beautiful reminder of the unlimited possibilities that are waiting for me.

My faith encourages me to release
the power of God within me.

Day 40

—◆—

Not knowing when the dawn will come,
I open every door.
—Emily Dickinson

HOME BLESSING God, You bless my home with love and peace, joy and happiness. May all who enter my home immediately feel welcome and at ease.

More than just bricks and mortar, wood and steel, my home is a place of peace where I can relax and be immersed in the comfort and company of family and friends.

I know that Your presence is here, God, for I feel Your strength and love within me in every moment of the day. And I pray that all who cross the threshold of my home will experience this same feeling of peace from knowing You in their lives.

My home—a haven for all who live in it and visit it— is built on a firm foundation of love and peace. Thank You, God, for blessing me and all who enter my home.

God blesses my home.

Day 41

—◆—

Have a compassionate heart
towards all creatures.
—Ko Hung

HARMONY My commitment to live, work, and communicate in harmony with others is one of the greatest gifts I can give to my family, my friends, and my co-workers. And because I give it freely and unconditionally, this gift from the heart gives increasingly back to me. I give love and consideration to others, and these qualities return to me—from many different people.

Harmonious relationships are always possible because the presence of God is within all people and all situations.

I am kind to my family, my friends, and all living things, knowing that they, too, are creations of God. I honor the presence of God when I honor each and every one of God's creations.

I give the gift of harmony freely and unconditionally.

Day 42

—◆—

Treat people as if they were what they ought to be,
and you help them to become what they are capable
of being.—Johann Wolfgang von Goethe

SPECIAL DAY

Parents know how good it feels to be able to give their children whatever enriches their lives. Holidays and birthdays are joyous occasions not only for the children but also for the adults who have worked so hard to give their children these truly special days. What love and satisfaction these parents must feel, and how truly blessed they are.

As my divine parent, God has prepared the way of abundance for me. I am God's beloved child, and I have been given everything I could ever need to enrich me and my life—spiritually and materially. Blessings such as I have never before seen or imagined are here for me today! God is blessing me with the ability to make today and every day a special day!

I gratefully accept the blessings of today.

Day 43

—◆—

*The greatest mistake you can make in life is
to be continually fearing that you will make one.*
—Ellen Hubbard

AMAZING LIFE

Life is amazing! And what makes it so amazing is that the spirit of God within me is yearning to be lived out through me as unqualified love and caring.

I can easily imagine that the single flower that has grown up through a tiny crack in the sidewalk is bursting to shout, "I made it!"

When I hug a tearful toddler who needs to be held, there is a surge of love and caring between us—so much, in fact, that I feel as blessed as the child needing comfort.

All around me I see evidence of divine life—life that was made for sharing, life that continually urges me to let it find expression through me.

The spirit of God within me is life!

Day 44

— ♦ —

*This could be such a beautiful world
if we could all care just a little more.*
—Rosalind Welcher

REACHING OUT Even though I am aware of the presence of God within me, there are times when I feel a need to reach out to another for help.

God is present in every person, so whenever God is acknowledged as the source of all love and understanding by people reaching out for help or to help, great things are possible.

There is a great invisible bond formed by people reaching out to other people. Each new connection on the soul level brings more people together in love and understanding.

I remember the people who have helped me and the people whom I have helped. We share a spiritual connection that can never be broken, a faith and hope that, person by person, blesses the world community.

**I reach out in spiritual awareness
to bless and be blessed.**

Day 45

—◆—

*May the road rise to meet you. May the wind always be
at your back. May the sun shine warm upon your face,
the rains fall soft upon your fields and, until we meet
again, may God hold you in the palm of His hand.*
—*Irish blessing*

**PRAYER
FOR
LOVED
ONES**

I bless my friends and family in my
prayers each day, sending them my
most caring thoughts:

"Dear ones, we have been brought
together through a divine plan, and I make a firm
commitment to be a blessing to you—just as you have
been a blessing to me.

"My words to you will always be loving and kind,
and I will support you in letting your inner light shine.
God loves you and so do I; I trust that you feel this love
encircling you.

"I feel such joy in knowing you, and each day I pray
that you experience unlimited peace and love in your
life. I am at ease about you, for I know you are cared for
by God."

**Dear ones, in my prayers I bless you
with love and faith.**

Day 46

—◆—

For the Children

Hello God,

It's fun to look at the stars that come out at night—all shiny and bright and filling up the sky. They remind me of what my mom and dad told me: You put twinkling stars in the sky to wink at me and remind me that You are near.

Then I think about all the kids in all the countries around the world—all looking at the same sky that I am. I know that You must be with them, too, causing the stars to wink at them.

When I look really hard and use my imagination, I can almost see that You are holding up the sky—keeping the stars in place so that I will never forget how much You love me. Your love must be bigger than the whole universe.

When I go to bed tonight, God, I'm going to look out my window and count the stars. And before I fall asleep, I'll send You a big wink that says, "I love You!"

Day 47

—◆—

Not only is God always with us as our help and strength,
but He is with us as the Spirit in us that inspires us
to reach out, to press forward.—Martha Smock

COMFORT AND STRENGTH God, in the sacred atmosphere of prayer, I become totally aware of You. And in this awareness, I receive comfort and strength.

You know the concerns that are on my mind and heart. Your presence in my life fills a void that could never be replaced by anyone or anything.

If my loved ones are troubled, I naturally want to help and encourage them. But sometimes I may feel as if my words or actions are not enough. So I turn to You for strength. You guide me in what I say and do, and You shelter my dear ones in Your love.

God, You encourage me when I need hope and guide me when I seem lost. You are my comfort and my strength.

I turn to God for comfort and strength.

Day 48

—◆—

*Until he extends his circle of compassion
to all living things, man will not himself find peace.*
—Albert Schweitzer

COMPASSION

King Solomon's wisdom served him well when two women claimed to be the mother of the same infant. Deciding who should have the child called for great wisdom, but it was the great compassion for the child by one of the women that revealed the true mother to Solomon (1 Kings 3:16–28).

Compassion is the kind of caring for and about others that has the spirit of God as its source. When I am compassionate with loved ones, friends, and neighbors, I am calling on the power of God to inspire me. Being compassionate, I reach to the core of my being for spiritual understanding and love, and these qualities support and encourage the best in me and from me, the best in others and from others.

**My compassionate nature springs
from the spirit of God within me.**

Day 49

—◆—

*The environment that people live in is the environment
that they learn to live in, respond to, and perpetuate.*
—Ellen Swallow Richards

**WORLD
COMMUNITY**
A picture of Earth taken by
satellite gives little indication that this
planet is inhabited by billions of
people who are each unique and
special in their own way.

I share a global home that God has given to all, and
through the abundance of planet Earth, all physical
needs can be met. Yet in order for life to flourish, an
atmosphere of order and peace needs to be maintained.

Peace is not something I can hold in my hands and
then pass on to other people. Peace is a feeling that is
born within the soul and multiplies when it is shared
through thoughts and actions—one person to another.

My world is a community of people who have God
as the one and only source of their life. Peace in the
world begins with me and depends on each and every
individual.

**Peace begins with me and spreads
throughout the world.**

Day 50

—◆—

*You will find as you look back upon your life
that the moments when you have truly lived
are the moments when you have done things
in the spirit of love.—Henry Drummond*

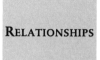
RELATIONSHIPS

Love and faith form the foundation
of my relationship with God—and
they are a good basis for all my
relationships.

If I am a parent, I know that I have been blessed with
a sacred trust. I understand that children are not my
possessions. My role in their lives is to be there for
them and to love them. And I do love my children and
all children.

True friendship is based on trust and understanding,
and I develop these qualities in my relationship with
God. Just as God does not condemn me, I do not
condemn others. Just as God gives me the freedom to
make my own decisions, I give others the freedom to
make their own decisions. My deepening relationship
with God enhances all my relationships.

**My loving, trusting relationship with God
is a model for my relationships with others.**

Day 51

—◆—

A baby is God's opinion
that the world should go on.
—Carl Sandburg

NEVER ALONE

If I am feeling lonely, I may pick up the telephone and speak with a loved one who lives far away. Even though we are separated by thousands of miles, the voice of my loved one coming from the phone sounds as clear and comforting as if that person were in the room with me. That connection frees me from feeling lonely.

The truth is that I am never really alone, for God's loving presence is always with me. Although I may miss family and friends, I know that we have an eternal spiritual connection. A prayer can reach out from us and to us, uniting us faster than any telephone connection or means of transportation.

I am one in spirit with God and with my loved ones. As I pray for them and they pray for me, we participate in a sacred activity that unites us as one spirit in God.

I am united with God and with my loved ones
in a heartfelt spiritual connection.

Day 52

—◆—

*My soul is painted like
the wings of butterflies.*
—*Freddie Mercury*

**DIVINE
PARTNERSHIP**
As much as I love my family and friends, sometimes they are not the ones with whom I feel most comfortable talking about my challenges and concerns. So where do I turn?

Talking to God, I will always be listened to without being judged. God loves me, and I am enfolded in the love and peace of God at all times. God gives instant relief to my troubled soul, and I feel uplifted.

Reaching out to God in faith, I enter into a divine partnership that blesses me spiritually and emotionally. The power of God within me heals and guides me, and my faith increases each day as I take part in a sacred partnership of the soul.

**Through my faith and my prayers,
I am living a partnership with God.**

Day 53

—◆—

Somewhere over the rainbow
Skies are blue
And the dreams that you dare to dream
Really do come true.
—E. Y. Harburg

RAINBOWS The beauty of a rainbow arching across the sky is a wonder that captures everyone's attention. Yet such a stunning sight is composed of apparently colorless droplets of water—until they are caught in the light of the sun.

Each droplet that makes up the rainbow remains a particle of water. The physical aspect of it has not changed; but the addition of sunlight has caused all to see its radiant potential.

I, too, can reflect light in my life—the beautiful light of God. And as I reflect the peace and joy that come through knowing the presence of God, my true potential can be seen. I am a rainbow of love and faith in God's world.

I live in the light and love of God.

Day 54

———◆———

The outer conditions of a person's life will always
be found to reflect their inner beliefs.
—James Allen

ENFOLDED IN LOVE I may wonder about the safety of my friends and family when they are away from me, but I know that wherever they go and whatever they do, God is with them to love them and to direct them.

This same assurance is true for me. I can never be away from God's loving presence. God is the strength I need to keep going, the light that shines before me to guide me safely along my way.

So whatever I face today, I can be certain that God will see me through. God's love will never fail me, and knowing this gives me a true sense of security.

Wherever I go and whatever I do, God's presence is with me. In that holy presence, I am enfolded in love.

Wherever I go, I am enfolded in God's
loving presence.

DAILY WORD FOR FAMILIES

Day 55

—◆—

*Nothing great was ever achieved
without enthusiasm.
—Ralph Waldo Emerson*

LIFE

God, Your life is within me and is right now moving through every muscle, organ, and cell of my body. Powerful, divine life maintains and restores the wholeness of my body.

You are the very spirit of life that revitalizes me. I feel so alive, so aware of the world around me and the radiance of Your life-giving presence in everyone and everything.

God, I am thankful that Your presence infuses me with life! My heart beats with the rhythm of divine life, and I am in tune with Your life-giving spirit.

I am open to the unimpeded flow of life throughout my mind and body. Each beat of my heart proclaims life and creates the tempo for a song of eternal life.

The spirit of God infuses me with life!

Day 56

---◆---

*Never give up, for that is just the place
and time that the tide will turn.*
—Harriet Beecher Stowe

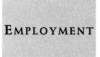

EMPLOYMENT

It is not what I do that defines me but who I am. And I am a creation of the Creator of all there is or ever will be. I honor God when I honor myself as God's creation.

I never think of myself as anything less than God's own capable and wise creation. If I don't currently have the education or skills that qualify me for a job, I can learn on the job or in a classroom.

I know, too, that when I am enthusiastic about what I do, I am better at doing it. Because I feel confident about myself, I encourage others to have confidence in me—whether it's during a job interview or right in the midst of a project.

There is right employment for me, and one of the richest rewards in doing anything is to experience joy in doing it.

I am a capable, wise creation of God.

Day 57

—◆—

The whole point of getting things done
is knowing what to leave undone.
—Lady Stella Reading

SWEET PROMISE If I am dreading an upcoming project or event, I will more than likely feel great relief—not a great sense of accomplishment—once it's over. Yet even before a task is complete, I can experience serenity of the soul by turning to God in prayer.

In silence, I fully experience what peace is. The concerns that I may have carried with me are gone, lifted away by the power of prayer. Any physical or mental exhaustion I may have felt is now replaced with strength and confidence. God has whispered a sweet promise of hope and renewal in my soul, and I bask in the peace I receive from this promise.

Because my soul has been soothed by the peace of God, I look forward to what lies ahead, and I relish the experiences that I have been given.

My soul is soothed by the peace of God.

Day 58

—◆—

Tenderness is the grace of the heart,
as style is the grace of the mind.
—*May Sarton*

TENDER TOUCH

Sweet Spirit, in the innermost depths of my being, I feel Your loving presence. Like a gentle breeze on a warm summer day, Your tender touch soothes me and ushers me to a place of tranquillity.

In this quiet place, I explore the recesses of my soul and bring any feeling of sorrow or despair into the light of Your presence. Here I release all burdens: I let go of the hurts; I let go of the worries; I let go of any feelings of bitterness that would keep me from experiencing Your love.

As I let go of any concerns, Your love rushes in to comfort me, assuring me that I am safe. In Your loving presence, God, I am filled with happiness and a peace that is beyond compare.

I am comforted by God's tender touch.

Day 59

—◆—

We must do all in our power to educate the public,
for I believe that in the end, only a change of heart
is really effective.—Ruth Harrison

REFRESHED

A quick inventory of the expression on my face and the level of tension in my body is a powerful reminder of how my thoughts affect me emotionally and physically.

When I think loving, happy thoughts, I cannot keep a smile from my lips. When I let my thoughts take a detour down a negative path, my face and my whole body tense.

I save wear and tear on my body and emotions by immediately eliminating any thoughts that may cause me emotional or physical pain. One major negative to watch for and eliminate is an unforgiving thought.

Forgiving myself and others refreshes me with feelings of love and compassion. I forgive because I understand how good forgiveness can feel and be!

As I forgive, I am refreshed by feelings
of love and compassion.

Day 60

Circle of Love

A family of loving, supportive people is so much more than a certain number or kind of individuals. Every person in our lives—family, friends, co-workers, and teachers—makes up an extended family that blesses all who are a part of it.

Let us give thanks for every person who has touched our lives, for each has made a contribution to our awareness of the goodness of God in us and in others.

Every kind gesture to us and from us is a true reflection of the spirit of God within us. Every loving thought goes out from us in ever-increasing waves to affect the great circle of love and life in miraculous ways.

Thank You, God, for the loving people who make up the circle of love that is life!

When he established the heavens, I was there,
when he drew a circle on the face of the deep,
when he made firm the skies above . . .
I was beside him . . . and I was daily his delight.
—Proverbs 8:27–30

NEVER TOO LATE
BY LYNDA WELLS

I n 1939, when the Andrews Sisters launched their singing career, the world was on the brink of a world war. Three young sisters—Maxene, Patty, and LaVerne—entered the world arena singing a combination of jive, jazz, and harmony. They brought the joy of upbeat rhythm and songs to people going through great personal sacrifice—separation from family and loved ones, and even death.

Forty years later, Maxene launched a solo career at an age when most people retire. She was my godmother from childhood and my adopted second mother in adulthood, and I felt as if God had brought the two of us together out of a sea of people. Being her manager was my way of helping her contribute her life back to the world.

Although both our lives had been based on Christian beliefs, we had never had a personal relationship with God. But one day, when we attended a church service with friends, that changed. During this inspiring service, both Maxene and I suddenly began to cry. Our tears produced a cleansing, and then we felt God's unconditional love.

Our lives turned around after that experience.

Maxene tried her act out in New York City, and she was a huge success. She did some television work, which led to a major show for PBS with June Allyson and Van Johnson called *GI Jive*. Then she started doing concerts and singing with symphony orchestras all over the world, remaining active right up until her death in 1995.

Right after finishing an off-Broadway show called *Swingtime Canteen*, we vacationed with friends on Cape Cod. The night before she died, I went in to tell her good night. Holding up her *Daily Word* magazine, which was always with her, she said, "Here, let me read today's word to you." This is what she read: "God, whatever I'm going through, I remember that You are my creator, that You have given me life. . . . In life, there is love—a circulation of love from You to me and from me to others. I love for the pure joy of loving."

The next evening, Maxene had a major heart attack. At the hospital, she was put on a ventilator. I knew she would not want to be kept alive artificially, and the cardiologist promised to remove her from life support in 24 hours if she had not improved.

I thought of friends who had been with loved ones going through the experience of death. They said how important it was to release them and give them permission to go.

I walked into the coronary-care room and up to

Maxene's bedside. Touching her arm, I said, "Honey, if you see the light, go to it. It's okay." All of a sudden, a nurse and the doctor, who were standing at the foot of the bed, gasped.

"Her heartbeat is not showing on the monitor," the doctor said, then started giving instructions to the nurse.

"Don't do anything!" I said. Running out into the hall, I summoned some friends who were waiting there. We formed a circle around Maxene, laid hands on her, and prayed. I knew then that the mercy and grace of God were reaching out to Maxene. I felt at peace about her.

We all hope that death never comes to a person until that person is ready for it. I believe Maxene knew how much she was loved and appreciated—all over the world. At 79 years of age, she was being pursued by people who wanted her to perform.

She had been such an inspiration to so many people—for her own generation and for many generations after. In fact, we had learned that the average age of her audience was 23 years old.

I was one of four people who made up Maxene's "chosen" family of children. The others were Steve, a foster son, and Aleda and Peter, her two other adopted children. We were a blessed family.

Maxene had a great career that evolved into a ministry of joy and love to others. People would grab her hands, look into her eyes, and give her a hug, saying,

"What is this light I see in you?" I believe that what they saw was the spirit of God shining from her. It shone in her face, and it absolutely transformed her performances.

Before every performance, Maxene, her musical director Phil Campanella, and I would hold hands in a circle and pray. She never performed without first asking God to minister to her. Maxene taught me and so many others that it is never too late to live life fully. It is never too late to let the light of God shine from within out into the world.

Day 61

—◆—

*There is nothing so lovely and enduring in the regions
which surround us, above and below, as the lasting peace
of a mind centered in Christ.*—Yogi Vasishtha

PERSONAL COMPANION As I work, play, relax, or travel, I experience the presence of God as my constant companion. Because I am aware of God's presence wherever I go and in whatever I do, I am focused on what enriches my life. I listen for and hear even the slightest whisper of a thought concerning my well-being or the well-being of others.

Before I make any travel plans or find myself having to venture out in adverse weather, I first acknowledge that the presence of God goes with me. What greater experience could I have than knowing the presence of God as an all-powerful spirit that accompanies me everywhere and always?

God is my personal, faithful companion.

Day 62

—◆—

There are two ways of spreading light:
to be the candle or the mirror that reflects it.
—Edith Wharton

TIME FOR SHARING Anytime of the year can be a perfect time for giving and receiving, a time of sharing with friends and loved ones. What better time could there be than now for me to acknowledge the spirit of God within that unites me with all people in a sacred bond?

I recognize my blessings: I give thanks for the grace of God that has made me truly prosperous. Divine love blesses me always, for the spirit of God is with me now and forever.

It is true: I live in the wonder and joy of God every day. I do so by remembering that every moment is a gift from God, a gift of unlimited possibilities and everlasting peace.

Every moment is a time to acknowledge and share an awareness of the spirit of God within.

Day 63

—◆—

The doors of wisdom are never shut.
—Benjamin Franklin

GUIDING LIGHT   If I am driving in unfamiliar territory, I might use a road map as my guide. In my journey through life, God is my guide in making wise decisions and choosing right actions.

I know that the very spirit of God within me is my instant, constant guidance in all matters and at all times. In everything—from a seemingly insignificant decision to an apparently monumental turning point in life—I know that God's spirit within me is wisdom, strength, and courage I can call upon.

The light of wisdom and understanding shines brightly within me, gently teaching me and guiding me forward in a spiritually enriched life.

The light of God shines brightly from within me,
guiding and enriching me with wisdom.

Day 64

—◆—

Cherish your human connections:
your relationships with friends and family.
—Barbara Bush

FEAST FOR THE SOUL

God enriches me with a feast for my soul that I can enjoy every day of my life. My daily feast includes the nourishment of God's love for me and God's love being expressed in my relationships.

My thoughts are never far from my family and friends and how our times together enrich my life. I feel such gratitude for the beauty and wonder of each of my loved ones and for all of God's creation.

I give thanks for the blessings of joy and peace in my interactions with family and friends. As I learn to savor the love and joy and peace of life, I am truly ready to accept the miracles of God as a feast for my soul.

> **God's blessings of love and joy and peace**
> **in my relationships are a rich feast for my soul.**

Day 65

—◆—

*Plant a kernel of wheat and you reap a pint; plant
a pint and you reap a bushel. Always the law works to
give you back more than you give.—Anthony Norvell*

**GIFT
OF LIFE**

A circle of joy unites the giver and
the receiver of a gift. And at times I
may become more caught up in the
experience of giving than of receiving.
So today I renew my joy by being open to receiving.

As an enthusiastic receiver, I accept so much more
than the gift itself. I welcome the giver as well as the gift
and receive the added blessings of love and
thoughtfulness that accompany the gift.

And, oh, what joy I feel in accepting the gift of life
and the renewal of life each day! I am truly grateful and
embrace the precious gift wholeheartedly.

**I am a joyful receiver of the gift of life
and all other gifts from God.**

Day 66

—◆—

For peace of mind, we need to resign
as general manager of the universe.
—Larry Eisenberg

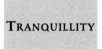

TRANQUILLITY I feel such peace in knowing that God will take care of me and everything that concerns me. With this understanding, I release worries rather than let them become a burden I carry with me.

My peace also comes from joyful news—God is my creator, and the peace and wonder of God's spirit are within me. My awareness of these truths opens the way to inner peace. Faith assures me that true serenity is my divine inheritance.

The peace of God within me is more than a state of mind—it is a state of being. And by living my life by drawing from the pool of tranquillity that always abides within me, I am being the peace of God in my world.

I am filled with the beauty and tranquillity
of Spirit Divine.

Day 67

---◆---

You can change your beliefs so they empower your dreams and desires. Create a strong belief in yourself and what you want.—Marcia Wieder

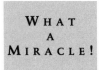
WHAT A MIRACLE!

What a miracle it would be if just for a moment there were no pain, no heartache, no discord in all the world! Everyone would live fully and love unconditionally.

The truth is that I can contribute to such a miracle! I can do it by focusing on the presence of God within me. By doing so I open myself to a fresh outpouring of life, love, and comfort from God.

Today, I recommit myself to a greater awareness of God and the enabling power God gives me. As others see the glorious change in my self-confidence and serenity, they, too, are sparked by a surge of spiritual awareness that springs forth to enrich their lives and to better the world.

I enrich my life and the lives of others with spiritual awareness.

Day 68

———◆———

We must be steady enough in ourselves to be open and to let the winds of life blow through us, to be our breath, our inspiration.—Mary Caroline Richards

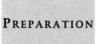

PREPARATION Whether I am working on a home improvement project or creating a meal for my family, I want to be prepared. So I make certain that I have the items and the time I need to complete whatever I am doing and to do it well.

I realize that preparation for my life—for the days and years ahead—is vitally important, too. But I don't worry about the future, for God has already prepared me to both receive and share blessings throughout my life.

I open my mind and heart to God's will and guidance. God guides me so that my vision is expanded to include a vast horizon. And in the process, I understand that I will be prepared to do my own part in bringing more love and peace to my family, to my community, and to the world.

Today, God is preparing me for the even greater blessings of tomorrow.

———— 79 ————

Day 69

—◆—

You are today where your thoughts have brought you;
you will be tomorrow where your thoughts take you.
—James Allen

HEALING PROCESS

Healing is more than the restoration of physical health. It is an ongoing process of my thoughts. So I keep my attitudes and beliefs about myself and the way I want to live in line with my true nature, my spiritual identity.

Whatever form my healing needs may take—healing of mind or body—I acknowledge that they spring forth from God's spirit within me. Then I let my thoughts affirm the truth about me: God created me to be healthy and whole!

Holding on to an image of wholeness when my body is telling me something else may be difficult. Yet I know that God created me for life, so I remain resolute in my belief that I am being healed! Today is just the first day in a whole new life for me!

God created me to be healthy and whole!

Day 70

—◆—

*I am optimistic and confident in all that
I do. I affirm only the best for myself and others. . . .
I fill my mind with positive, nurturing,
and healing thoughts.—Alice Potter*

**SPIRITUAL
FULFILLMENT**

There is a constant rhythm of life emanating from me. The hum of my spiritual energy blends with a whole chorus of order sounding around the world—a chorus of life-giving thanks that God is in charge and maintaining an order that blesses all people.

As a beloved child of God, I am not alive by chance; I am living in this time and place by divine appointment. I am here to live life as the divine creation I am. I can because divine order always supports me in moving forward in spiritual fulfillment.

My life has divine purpose because God has established order within me and within the world that I call home.

**I am spiritually fulfilled and living in
an orderly world of God's creation.**

Day 71

---◆---

Rule #1: Don't sweat the small stuff.
Rule #2: It's all small stuff.
—Michael Mantell

RELEASE Mental and physical well-being go hand in hand. Knowing this, I remind myself not to worry about situations or allow stress to build inside me. I feel good about helping promote my own health.

By remaining calm and peaceful, I am helping to keep my blood pressure in a healthy range and my muscles relaxed. I have peace of mind in knowing that I can quickly and easily turn all matters over to God.

I make each day a commitment to trusting in divine wisdom and allowing God to guide me and free me from all concern. I know that no problem is too great for God. So I release any feelings of anxiety into God's care. As I let go, I feel a tremendous sense of relief and freedom, and my body and mind benefit.

I let go and let God, trusting in divine wisdom.

Day 72

—◆—

Dedicate yourself to the good you deserve and desire for yourself. Give yourself peace of mind. You deserve to be happy. You deserve delight.—Mark Victor Hansen

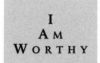

I AM WORTHY

God, right now, in this moment, I realize that You are here with me. I know the truth about myself: I am Your creation, Your child. Any feelings of unworthiness are washed away by the joy I experience in Your presence.

I love You, God. Although I may wonder how I could possibly be worthy of Your love, I embrace it with such gratitude that I discover how to love myself. I understand that what I love about me is the pure, compassionate essence of life and love that You are within my soul.

God, I live my life in celebration of Your presence within me and all around me. I feel worthy, and out of this awareness a new, more confident me arises. I dedicate myself to being more of a blessing to the world.

I am a child of God—worthy of being blessed and of being a blessing.

Day 73

—◆—

You have powers you never dreamed of.
You can do things you never thought you could do.
There are no limitations in what you can do except
the limitations of your own mind.—Darwin P. Kingsley

DISCOVERY

My perspective changes when others, especially children, admire a familiar scene or circumstance that I have begun to take for granted. When I allow myself to see the promise they see, I, too, discover a world filled with possibilities!

The world has not changed, but I have taken a new look at the world already before me. When I changed my perspective, I began to see the world as God created it to be, and what a glorious vision that is!

Every day and every person has potential and promise. There is always an exciting new world just waiting to be explored. With love and appreciation, I see the opportunities around me. I give thanks to God for such a beautiful world—a world of great possibilities.

I am continually discovering a world
of great possibilities.

Day 74

—◆—

Do not worry about whether or not the sun will rise.
Be prepared to enjoy it.
—Pearl Bailey

SAFE AND SECURE

Young children look to their parents and other caregivers to provide an atmosphere that is both safe and nurturing to their individual growth.

As an adult, this desire may continue as I expect others to make me feel loved and safe. Yet it is only when I learn to trust in myself and in God's presence within me that I will ever feel the security I seek.

God's loving presence is the firm foundation on which I build true security in my life. I know that God is always with me, so it naturally follows that God's wisdom and love can be the mainstay of my existence, if only I will let them be. In truth, God's love provides the very shelter of security in which I thrive.

God's loving presence is my true security.

Day 75

—◆—

In him was life, and the life
was the light of all people.
—John 1:4

I BELIEVE! At one time, I may have felt that life was one long search to know the meaning and purpose of my existence. However, now I know that my search was not about me; it was *for* God.

I know because I find the peace I desire through my quiet talks with God. As I look at the beauty of the natural wonders around me, I feel God's presence. I understand that the presence of God is beyond shape or form because God is everywhere.

I grow in wisdom and learn from the experiences I have. I discover that my journey is not to a special time or place in order to find God, for God is with me all the time. The peace I find and the beauty of God I witness are all a part of what I take in through my senses, all a part of who I am and who I will always be.

Dear God, I do believe in You!

Day 76

For the Children

Hello God,

Is it true that no matter where I am or what I am doing, You are with me? It is? I'm glad that even when I'm on vacation and far, far away, You are still with me.

I talk to You all the time, God. And I know that You hear what I say. Today, I want to say thanks for all of the fun things You have given me to play with. I really like climbing those trees that You made. And the grass is just right for curling my bare toes in. Every time I hear a bird singing a song to me, I think of You, God, and I know that You are near.

Every time I look in a mirror, I think of You, God. When I smile at the mirror, I think of You smiling at me, and it makes me so happy! Thanks for all of the great stuff You give me and for loving me so much that You never leave me alone.

Day 77

—◆—

Grace has been defined as the outward expression
of the inward harmony of the soul.
—William Hazlitt

REFLECTION OF GOD

I know that the grace of God is active in my life, for I see it, feel it, and live in its loving atmosphere every day.

I see God's grace reflected in the faces of my loved ones. Grace materializes as the blessing of food that nourishes me and a home that is a haven of peace.

I feel God's grace as love and joy in my heart. Such feelings are greatly intensified when I go into a time of prayer with my Creator.

I live in God's grace. Grace assures me that I will never be alone, for God is with me always. I am willing to share the message of our divine heritage with every other child of God. I do this by being an expression of God's grace in the world.

I see and feel the grace of God that is continually reflected around me.

Day 78

— ◆ —

*I've always thought that people need to feel good
about themselves, and I see my role as offering support
to them, to provide some light along the way.*
—Diana, Princess of Wales

**LOVING
CARE**

Knowing how to help people—even family and lifelong friends—can seem a mystery at times. When loved ones are hurting, I want to ease their pain. I want them to live healthy, happy, and fulfilled lives, but I cannot make all this happen for them.

There is much I can do, however. When I hold someone's hand, a bond of love and comfort is created that blesses us both. Listening quietly to children and adults who need to be heard is an investment in their well-being.

I pray for others and remind them that they are unique, precious creations of God. In the role of a loving caregiver—from the simple act of tying a child's shoelaces to the complete responsibility for adults who can no longer care for themselves—I give care that is inspired by the spirit of God within me.

The loving care I give is inspired by God.

Day 79

— ♦ —

*Too often the opportunity knocks, but by the time
you push back the chain, push back the bolt, unhook
the locks, and shut off the burglar alarm, it's too late.*
—Rita Coolidge

OPPORTUNITIES I have something in common with all people: the open door to opportunities that is available from God. I know that, with God, all things are possible, and as I listen to divine wisdom and follow the guidance I receive, all things become possible for me.

With God guiding my way, I put behind me whatever it is that has tended to limit me—whether it is what family and friends have said about my capabilities or society's preconceived ideas of what I can achieve.

Ingenuity and creativity spark my imagination and show me the opportunities that await. God lifts me to new heights, and I am able to soar on the wings of faith and accept every opportunity as a blessing.

I gratefully accept every opportunity God offers me.

Day 80

—◆—

The weak can never forgive. Forgiveness is
the attribute of the strong.
—Mahatma Gandhi

**PERFECT
LOVE**

When children are first learning to ride a bicycle, training wheels give them a chance to experience balance. And I consider forgiveness a similar aid in my spiritual growth. Forgiveness is a kind of training wheel that enables me to know how it feels to be in harmony with others.

When I practice being nonjudgmental and remaining totally focused on the love of God, I am opening the way to harmony and understanding. In time, when I have learned not to pass judgment on the actions of someone else, I will no longer need to forgive, for I will have nothing to forgive.

If others have done or said something that upsets me, I bless them and go on my way. I am secure in the truth of my being: I am an expression of God's perfect love.

I am an expression of God's perfect love.

Day 81

———◆———

I could have traveled many paths that are interesting and perhaps more elaborate, but the simplicity of the path I chose still affects me: God is good.—Mary L. Kupferle

GOD'S WILL

I may hear about someone who has gone through an incredible challenge and now feels that the challenge turned out to be a blessing. If I am going through such an experience, I can maintain a positive attitude when I remember that every challenge is an opportunity in disguise.

With every circumstance, I am growing, for I am learning more about myself and what I am capable of achieving or overcoming. Fortified with the power and wisdom of God, I face each day with optimism and strength.

With God, every moment is a new beginning, a new opportunity to start over. No matter what has happened in the past, I know that what is to come holds promise—not because of my will, but because I am open to the wisdom of God's will.

Not my will, but God's be done.

Day 82

——◆——

Sometimes the most important thing in a whole day
is the rest we take between two deep breaths,
or the turning inward in prayer for five short minutes.
—Etty Hillesum

PRAYER OF FAITH Thank You, God, for blessing my dear ones and filling them with Your love. Wherever they go and wherever they may be, they are surrounded by Your mighty presence. In Your care, they will always find their way.

No matter how rough the road may become in their journeys through life, You are with them to guide and inspire them.

Your strength sustains them through every challenge. With faith in You, they will find that they can keep going, that they can be triumphant in whatever they do.

You inspire them and give them the support and encouragement they need to be the unique expressions of light and love You created them to be.

I pray a prayer of faith for my loved ones.

Day 83

—◆—

Make all your friends feel there is something special in them. . . . Spend so much time improving yourself that you have no time left to criticize others. Be too big for worry and too noble for anger.—Christian D. Larsen

HEART-AND-SOUL CONNECTION God, sometimes when I feel sad or disappointed, I imagine myself being held in the warm embrace of Your unconditional love. I feel safe and peaceful. And the miracle of it is that, in this moment of solitude with You, I feel a heart-and-soul connection with the world.

This awareness lingers with me to become a part of my interactions with others. I intuitively sense what to do to encourage harmony between me and my loved ones. I know when to speak and when to listen—doing both with love and understanding.

Yes, God, my heart's desire is to express love and harmony in my world.

Through the love of God, I share a heart-and-soul connection with all people.

Day 84

—◆—

When it is a question of God's
almighty Spirit, never say, "I can't."
—Oswald Chambers

HAPPINESS IN GOD   Children are often asked by adults about their dreams for the future—what they want as a career when they grow up. When I think back to the way I may have responded to that question as a child, do I find that I have fulfilled my dreams?

I might or might not have followed through with my childhood goals. But when I think about what is truly important in my life, I know that goals or career choices are not what make me happy. My happiness is in God.

The way to true happiness was paved for me before I ever entered this life. All I need to do is realize that the answer to all my desires and needs has been, is, and always will be found in God. Happiness is an enrichment of my soul that comes from knowing the presence of God.

My happiness from knowing God enriches my soul.

Day 85

—◆—

Build a little fence of trust around today;
fill the space with loving deeds, and therein stay.
Look not through the sheltering bars upon tomorrow;
God will help thee bear what comes of joy and sorrow.
—Mary F. Butts

SECURITY

Feeling safe and secure is a tremendous benefit to me even in routine matters: I think clearly, give my full attention to whatever I am doing, and get a good night's sleep.

And I give thanks that I can trust God at all times—when I am traveling or at home, when I am fully awake and active, or when I retreat from all activity and give myself over to complete rest and sleep.

What security I feel because I trust God! Because I do, I am always open to what is best for me. I understand that my well-being is not based on meeting schedules and appointments. I am guided to go or stay, to rest or be active by the spirit of God within me. God is my peace, my wisdom, and my security.

God, I am secure in Your loving care.

Day 86

—◆—

The cause of freedom
is the cause of God.
—Samuel Bowles

FREE

How can I ever feel free when so much is expected of me? I may go to work, meetings, or classes, doing more and absorbing more each day. I may have full responsibility for taking care of my home and my children—plus other responsibilities that need my attention. Is it any wonder that I can become so caught up in what must be done that I begin to feel trapped?

The way to freedom is not in being any less responsible in caring about and for others. It is in knowing that I have freedom of Spirit, in realizing that I have a freedom that goes beyond the physical realm to a place in mind and heart where I am one with God. When I know this, I connect on a real and conscious level with the power of God.

Now that I know I am free, I live my freedom as the gift from God that it is.

With freedom of Spirit, I am free.

Day 87

—◆—

The Eskimos had fifty-two names for snow because it was important to them; there ought to be as many for love.
—Margaret Atwood

RADIATING LOVE God loves me with an everlasting love and accepts me just as I am. Basking in the warm glow of such unconditional love nourishes me. I rejoice in the new and vibrant being I am becoming each day.

God's love radiates from within me. Pouring forth from my heart and soul, divine love does a powerful work through me. Filled with joy and thanksgiving, I am the loving person God created me to be. Being loving is simple because a smile or a hug can be just as meaningful to someone as the most carefully chosen words I can speak.

With all my heart and soul, I share God's love with everyone in my life and remember to act in a kind and loving way toward all that God has created.

The love of God radiates within me and from me.

Day 88

*There is a calmness to a life lived
in gratitude, a quiet joy.*
—Ralph H. Blum

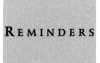

REMINDERS

It is often the little things—a letter, a card, a knickknack on a shelf—that remind me of good times and the joys I have accumulated over a lifetime of experiences.

I also have reminders of the good I have now, of the good I can experience in this very moment when I allow joy from within to shine forth. Daily reminders of my blessings are always there, just waiting for me to recognize them for what they are.

Listening to the gentle sounds of God's natural wonders, seeing the glow of a brightly smiling face, or feeling the touch of love when a child holds my hand are all God's blessings. They are precious reminders that God is always with me—a very real presence in my life.

Thank God for reminders of divine blessings.

Day 89

—◆—

The disciples went and did as Jesus had directed them. . . .
A very large crowd spread their cloaks on the road, and
others cut branches from the trees and spread them on
the road. The crowds that went ahead of him and that
followed were shouting, "Hosanna to the Son of David!"
—Matthew 21:6–9

KINDNESS

If I am looking for ways to be kinder to others, I remember the Golden Rule: "In everything do to others as you would have them do to you." (Matthew 7:12)

When I am with family and friends, I show my appreciation for their presence in my life and let them know that I value them. I give co-workers, fellow students, and strangers the same respect and kindness that I would like to receive from them.

I can readily offer my assistance to someone in need by listening and being understanding. Each investment I make in being loving and kind toward others will reap the benefit of a more loving and harmonious world for us all.

I am patient and kind.

Day 90

Circle of Love

We have been drawn together, as one family of God, in this place and at this time. It is not by happenstance that we are here—it is by the order of God that has ruled the universe since long before we became a part of this circle of life and love.

Everything that we do and say will, in some measure, affect this space and this time. So we act in loving ways and speak with loving tones, assuring ourselves that the imprints we leave on Earth will be positive ones that benefit future generations.

Our circle of love will continue—from person to person, city to city, country to country—until love spans the globe. We are one people united by God—and God is and always will be perfect love.

We must not, in trying to think about how we can make a big difference, ignore the small daily differences we can make which, over time, add up to big differences that we often cannot foresee.
—Marian Wright Edelman

DAILY WORD FOR FAMILIES

A Trusted Friend
by Bob Barker

hen I first met Dorothy Jo in high school, I had no idea that this chance meeting would lead to a wonderful partnership in marriage and in life.

Dorothy Jo often appeared on my television shows with me. So did other members of our family—our dogs and cats. So the people who watch my shows regularly probably know me and my family better than some of the people I know socially or professionally. I have never played a "role" on television. I have always just been Bob Barker. And what you see is what you get.

When my dear wife passed away, I lost my life-long companion and best friend. Trying to keep my days full, I devoted more time to working for animal protection and, in doing so, accumulated a houseful of animals.

Then one day, another chance meeting brought another dear friend and family member into my life. I was driving with a friend when we noticed a dog lying in the street. Stopping to investigate, we discovered that it was dead. Our attention was quickly diverted, however, by the sound of growling coming from the bushes at the side of the road. As we peered into the bushes, we saw a little dog—disheveled and obviously a stray. But this little dog had a heart as big as all outdoors, for he was protecting his friend's body.

Moved by this heroic stand, we attempted to coax the dog into my car, but he would not budge. Pondering the situation, we came up with a solution: We placed the body of the dead dog in the backseat of my car. Immediately the little dog raced from the bushes and jumped in. There he placed his head on his friend's body—still protecting and caring for him.

This little dog's courage and caring touched me so much that I told him, "You know, little fellow, anybody who's that filled with love and devotion deserves a good home, and you have one!" And he does. To this day, Federico, as I named him, has a place in my home and in my heart.

I thank God daily for the dear friends and loved ones who have been a part of my life—friends whom I have met by chance and loved for a lifetime—friends like Dorothy Jo and, of course, Federico.

Day 91

—◆—

A dog wags its tail with its heart.
—Martin Buxbaum

ANIMAL BLESSING I feel such joy when I think about my family and friends that I give thanks to God often for them.

But my gratitude does not stop with these people. I give thanks for every living thing, for each one has an important contribution to make. And I include pets in my prayers, for they are loyal helpers. What pleases them most seems to be whatever pleases the people they love. And this is an important lesson for each of us.

If I have a special pet in my life, I give thanks for the loyalty and loving companionship it gives to me. What a sacred friendship we have! I expand my vision to include every creature on Earth, knowing that each one serves its own special purpose.

I bless all God's creatures—large and small.

Day 92

—◆—

It is perhaps a more fortunate destiny to have a taste
for collecting shells than to be born a millionaire.
—Robert Louis Stevenson

MY SOURCE If I were to ask several people what *prosperity* means to them, I would receive several different answers, such as "abundance," "success," "opulence," "victory." Prosperity probably has as many different meanings as there are people, for prosperity is a state of consciousness. It is up to each individual to decide what it means in his own life.

As for me, of all the things I may acquire in my lifetime, none can equal the pleasure I receive from the love of God—something that no amount of money can buy.

My life is full of spiritual gifts. I receive and draw upon God's love, strength, wisdom, and assurance every day. Yes, I am prosperous, for God has given me the gifts of spirit. I am grateful for every chance to use them in wise and loving ways.

God is the source of all my prosperity.

Day 93

———◆———

In every community, there is work to be done. In every nation, there are wounds to heal. In every heart, there is the power to do it.—Marianne Williamson

LIGHTHOUSE OF PEACE

The attitude with which I start the day tends to set the tone for the whole day. So if I am feeling peaceful about myself and the world around me, I will be calm and relaxed as I deal with the pressures of daily life. Conversely, if I am upset about something, my feelings will affect not only how I relate to others but also how well I go about doing the most minor tasks.

Yet I know I can remain peaceful through any situation when I open my mind and heart to the peace that passes all understanding—the peace of God. God's spirit is within me, so God's peace is within me, too, just waiting for me to let it shine forth. Like the comforting glow of a lighthouse in the midst of a storm, God's peace shines out from me as a beacon of light and love for others.

The peace of God shines within me and from me.

Day 94

—◆—

The reality of any place is what its
people remember of it.
—Charles Kuralt

PLACE OF LOVE
What do I do on a daily basis to help create an environment of love in my home? I fill it with loving thoughts and words and actions. I bless each room with my prayers for harmony and understanding.

I do what I can to make my home a place of love and acceptance so that it is a safe harbor for those who live there or who stay for a few hours or a few days. In my prayers, I give thanks to God for the blessing of my home:

"Dear God, I know that You bless everyone who enters my home. I give thanks for the joy and companionship, the harmony and understanding that we share.

"God, thank You for blessing all who reside within and visit my home and for blessing my home with Your loving presence."

My home is a place of love, an environment
of harmony and understanding.

Day 95

—◆—

*I've never been one who thought the Lord should
make life easy; I've just asked Him to make me strong.*
—Eva Bowring

**TRUST
GOD**

Aloha is a Hawaiian word used both as a greeting and as a farewell. Surely such a word conveys hope that every parting will bring a reunion between loved ones.

There may not be one word that conveys the hope that for every ending there will be a new beginning, but it is true—there can be a new beginning! So if I am in the throes of change, I do not give up hope. My vision may be fuzzy, but it will become clearer.

A change in the family routine or finances—caused by children moving out or back in or by the ending of a relationship, school term, or job—may be an end to my current lifestyle. However, God will see me through. As I trust in God, that new beginning will come. As surely as the sun rises each morning, a new beginning will appear.

**I trust that God will see me through any change
and on to a new beginning.**

Day 96

—◆—

*Unknowingly, we plow the dust of stars, blown about us
by the wind, and drink the universe in a glass of rain.*
—Ihab Hassan

IMPORTANT LINK
Each expression of life on Earth has an impact on the environment in which it lives. From the shortest blade of grass to the mightiest oak tree, from the single-celled organism to the complex human being, all are links in the great circle of life that spans the globe.

As I give thanks for this beloved planet and bless it in my prayers, I am honoring God and all that God has created. I am working hand in hand with others to be an important link in God's love on Earth. Together, we are creating an environment in which harmony and peace will prevail.

How glorious is the beauty of this great planet that God created to sustain and nurture us! And how blessed I am to be a part of such a magnificent world!

**I am an important link in God's circle of life
that spans the globe.**

DAILY WORD FOR FAMILIES

Day 97

---◆---

Blessed are the peacemakers, for they
will be called children of God.
—Matthew 5:9

HEART'S DESIRE

Seed and wind were created for a harmonious partnership. The seed is willing to fly on the wind in order to find its home, a place to put down roots and produce new life. The wind, however, is equally willing to remain homeless, roaming the Earth and carrying seed after seed home.

People, too, were created for harmonious partnerships with each other. Although some of us differ in beliefs and appearances, we are of the same Spirit. Surely we, too, have been carried along by the breath of Spirit to be life, to bring new life to every area on Earth.

Wherever we live—in a house or an apartment, in one neighborhood or another, in one country or another—we can make our homes places of harmony and goodwill. This truly is the desire of our hearts, the fulfillment of our souls.

It is my heart's desire to live in harmony
with all people, with all life.

Day 98

—◆—

God is love; it is God's nature to give. God has been giving to us all our lives, throughout eternity.
—Russel W. Lake

GOD BLESSES ME

God, I may think I know exactly what I want or need from this day, but I am thankful that You bless me with so much more than I can envision.

I accept both the expected and unexpected blessings. When I have met an expectation of what I can do, I feel good about it. When I go over the top in accomplishing some goal, however, this is when I have a greater realization of You, a greater realization that You have given me understanding and strength to make a giant leap forward.

Acknowledging *You* more never makes me less. The more I let You live through me, the more I am capable of doing. Thank You, God, for blessing me in ways that are beyond my understanding. Each blessing enriches my life.

With each blessing from God, my life is enriched.

Day 99

—◆—

*Yes, I have doubted. I have wandered off the path,
but I always return. It is intuitive, an intrinsic, built-in
sense of direction. I seem always to find my way home.
My faith has waived but saved me.*—Helen Hayes

I WILL FOLLOW

I may think that following divine guidance leaves little for me to do, but just the opposite is true. It calls on me to make a commitment to follow God. This is a commitment to what is pure and sacred, to fulfilling God's will.

I confirm my commitment in prayer:

"God, I entrust myself and all that is in the past, in the present, and in the future to You. I know that from this commitment, I will discover greater understanding of You, of myself, and of my world.

"You offer me unlimited freedom and opportunities as well as courage and wisdom. God, I will follow wherever You guide me. Thank You, God, for Your way is the way of peace, love, and life."

God, wherever You guide me, I will follow.

Day 100
— ◆ —

No matter how unimportant you think you are, regardless
of how wrongly you think you have handled anything
in your life, how little faith you seem to have, or how
inadequate you feel, God loves you.—Mary L. Kupferle

ASSURANCE My most challenging moments are often the ones in which I feel prompted to re-evaluate who I am and what I really desire from a job, a relationship, or anything else in life. My most inspiring moments, however, come from knowing that God is always with me.

The spirit of God—the spirit of grace—leads me to a place in my mind and heart where I feel safe. I know without a doubt that God is with me and ready to help me begin again—regardless of what has happened in the past.

So where I am going or where I have been is not nearly as important as where I am now. Through God's loving grace, I am sure that I have all I need to be the *me* that is part of the divine plan.

Divine grace is the assurance that God
is always with me.

Day 101

◆

Those are the same stars, and that is the same moon,
that look down upon your brothers and sisters . . . though
they are ever so far away from us, and each other.
—Sojourner Truth

EMBRACING
LOVED
ONES

God, I understand that praying for family and friends is a powerful way of expressing my love for them. I turn from worrying about them to having faith in Your spirit moving through them to heal and guide them.

Every prayer is a message of love that uplifts others with thoughts of health and peace and prosperity. Each prayer for others is a reminder to me that You are a source of ever-renewing life within them. You are inner wisdom that gives them mastery over every challenge in life.

Although I may not always be able to reach out and embrace my loved ones physically, I can embrace them with love and faith through prayer. You, dear God, unite us in spiritual oneness.

I embrace my loved ones in faith-filled prayer.

Day 102

—◆—

We are not human beings on a spiritual journey.
We are spiritual beings on a human journey.
—Stephen R. Covey

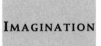

IMAGINATION Can you imagine a place where all people live in harmony with one another—a place where hunger does not exist, where discord is a thing of the past, where people genuinely care for one another and take care of one another?

Such a place can exist for all of us, because everything is possible through the power and presence of God.

All humankind shares a sacred kinship that flourishes when we recognize our ability to share our talents and time in ways that benefit one another. Sometimes it is a simple act of kindness that brings the greatest blessing.

Spirit will guide us to do whatever it takes to transform our dreams into a living reality.

With God, all things are possible.

Day 103

— ◆ —

You are an individualized expression of God,
and that is your only real characteristic.
—Mary-Alice and Richard Jafolla

CHILD OF GOD

I greet each day with joy and expectancy when I know the truth about me: *I am a beloved child of God.* Knowing that this is true, I am an example of joy and serenity to everyone I meet.

I am divine light in expression. In everything I do, God illuminates me, and I reflect that wisdom to others.

I am divine life in expression. God has imbued me with life and spirit. I have the assurance of knowing that I live every moment of life in the presence of God.

I am divine love in expression. With God as the source of perfect love, I express patience, kindness, and understanding to others.

God is my light, God is my life, God is my love. Being a child of God gives me a sacred purpose to fulfill in all areas of my life.

I am a beloved child of God.

Day 104

—◆—

Life is free-flowing. Life is the strong and never-ceasing current of activity which moves in, upon, and through all creation.—Sue Sikking

STREAM OF LIFE

Like a refreshing stream of life, the spirit of God flows throughout my body, soothing and healing me.

When I awaken each morning, I greet the day by affirming that throughout the night, Spirit has been preparing me for a new day. Right now, God's healing life is in every cell of my body, supplying me with energy. I have energy for the entire day, and some to spare.

I am grateful that even when I am least aware of it, the spirit of God continues to refresh me, bathing me in a healing flow that restores me—body and soul.

I am renewed. I feel refreshed and vitally alive. It is as if my spiritual battery has been recharged, and I enthusiastically embrace my day and my life.

The spirit of God flows within me as a healing stream.

Day 105
◆

In quiet places, reason abounds.
—Adlai E. Stevenson

STILLNESS OF MY SOUL In the stillness of my soul, I can feel God embracing me and reassuring me that I am loved. No words are spoken, for they are not needed. God communicates with me in a language that is inaudible to the human ear but that is clearly understood by my trusting soul.

This feeling of being loved and cherished stays with me throughout my day, my week, my lifetime. God's love for me is eternal. I am comforted, for I am loved.

In faith, I ask God for strength. In love, God reassures me that unlimited strength is always within me. Any concern is replaced with the assurance of divine comfort.

God is my source of everlasting peace and comfort.

Within the stillness of my soul,
I feel God's reassurance.

For the Children

Hello God,

I have been learning a lot about using my imagination. It's a gift You have given me, and I use it a lot. It's fun to imagine, and sometimes I do it when I need to be doing other things—like when I am in class but imagining I am roller-blading. My teacher says I am daydreaming, but it is more than that. With my imagination, I can feel, taste, smell, see, and hear things that I am only *thinking* about.

I wanted You to know how my imagination has *helped* me in school, too. When my class was reading about Africa, I could feel the heat of the African sun and hear the rustling of the dry grass as zebras walked on the plain. Then, as I read on, I saw a lion stand up from its resting place, stretch its neck, and open its mouth. Then I heard it roar! I was so interested in learning that I got an A on my test.

So, God, I guess this is a sort of thank-you prayer for my imagination. Sorry I took so long to let You know, but I am thankful.

Day 107

—◆—

If one is lucky, a solitary fantasy can
totally transform one million realities.
—Maya Angelou

FREEDOM

I imagine for a moment feeling completely free with the freedom of Spirit. I am free from worry, free from doubt, and free from any sense of insecurity.

Each thought I have about freedom of Spirit is released as a wave of peace that moves throughout my body. How relaxed I feel, how at peace I am with myself and with the world! Now I store this feeling of freedom in my memory so that I can claim it at any time.

I can claim freedom because I am completely unimpeded with the freedom of Spirit! God's loving spirit is always within me, and it is the spirit of God that will transform my life into one of everlasting peace. I am living a life of freedom!

My life is transformed through freedom of Spirit.

Day 108

—◆—

All I have seen teaches me to trust
the Creator for all I have not seen.
—Ralph Waldo Emerson

DIVINE CONNECTION I may see the familiar face of the person I am meeting in a crowd only to lose sight of it as people move about. Then, with total concentration, I search as if I am seeking that person with my whole being. Suddenly, the crowd opens and that face reappears.

Sometimes I may lose sight of my faith by letting fears and concerns crowd out my thoughts about it. However, God encourages me to have faith. So any time I feel a lack of faith, this is my cue to seek it out as I would a face in the crowd and rediscover my conscious connection with the spirit of God within me.

Yes, the spirit of God lives and loves through me, heals and comforts me. My faith in God moves me forward to receive blessing after blessing.

**My faith in God is my conscious connection
with the presence of God.**

Day 109

---◆---

For everyone who asks receives, and everyone who
searches finds, and for everyone who knocks, the door will
be opened.—Matthew 7:8

IN GOD'S CARE

What relief I feel knowing that God is with me at all times! My Creator is closer to me than the air I breathe and even more constant than the beat of my heart.

If I ever do feel lonely or lost, I imagine God taking my hand. A spiritual connection is always there, but when I am totally aware of it, I am blessed with peace. The touch of Spirit calms me and is more real to me than any experience I have ever had before or will ever have.

The spirit of God is always within me, surrounding me and going before me. Enfolded in the presence and care of God, I am safe and secure. I live from a spiritual awareness that enriches every thought I think and every experience I have.

Enfolded by Your presence, God, I am safe and secure.

Day 110

---◆---

What I admire in Columbus is not his having discovered a world but his having gone to search for it on the faith of an opinion.—A. Robert Turgot

WORK IN PROGRESS

On a daily basis, I set goals for myself—some are short-term, others are long-term. While setting these goals, I keep in mind that when I am truly allowing myself to be divinely directed, the outcome may not be what I had in mind. What is important is that all is according to a divine plan.

So rather than becoming frustrated with myself when I do not meet a goal, I take a mental step back and look at the situation again. Upon further reflection, I will see that it was, indeed, a learning experience for me and that I have actually made progress. Life is a huge classroom for learning, and I learn from all my experiences.

It's true: I am a divine work in progress. I welcome new experiences, for they are the tools that shape who I am and who I will be.

I am a divine work in progress!

Day 111

—◆—

Grandchildren are God's way
of compensating us for growing old.
—Mary H. Waldrip

GOD IS IN CHARGE

As parents and grandparents, uncles and aunts, one of the hardest things we may have to do is let go of our children so that they can learn something new. So whether we are taking the training wheels off a bike for a first-grader or handing over the car keys to a newly licensed driver, we may hesitate or feel unsure that what we are doing is right.

We do more, however, than take off the training wheels and let go of the car keys to allow the children to experience learning firsthand. We also pray for them, remaining strong and supportive, for we know that God is taking care of them even when we cannot.

Letting go and letting God be in charge, we are able to relax and enjoy the experience of watching our children and other loved ones discover more about what they are capable of doing and achieving.

Thank You, God, for taking care of loved ones.

Day 112

---◆---

A humble knowledge of thyself is a surer way
to God than a deep search after learning.
—Thomas à Kempis

KNOWING GOD

Do I ever feel as if something is missing from my life, that if only I look long enough or hard enough I would eventually find something that brings my life into focus?

Looking out into the world for answers will only get me so far and often adds to my confusion. It is in turning within, in seeking *God*, that I find the true desire of my heart.

So rather than searching for something on the outside, I change my focus to the inner realm where God and I are one. Here I find peace. Here I know God. I also know that God is ready to help me. Here I learn the true meaning of fulfillment.

My greatest blessing is in having
a greater awareness of God.

Day 113

—◆—

Every now and then, go away and have a little relaxation, for when you come back to your work, your judgment will be surer.—Leonardo da Vinci

REST

Healing of emotions, mind, and body is enhanced when I rest in the presence of God. When I stop thinking thoughts that wound me emotionally, when I stop some habit that is injurious to me physically or psychologically, I allow myself to heal.

Giving myself a rest, I become still and silent. In silence, my energy is no longer scattered in many directions; it all moves toward healing and renewing me.

As I let relationship conflicts rest, I allow time for a healing of whatever has caused a disagreement between me and others. Instead of reacting emotionally, I respond to the prompting of Spirit within me. When I am kind and loving, I encourage like responses from others. All kinds of healing occur when I rest in the silence with God.

Resting in silence with God, I am healed and restored.

Day 114

---◆---

To love what you do and feel that it matters—
how could anything be more fun?
—Katharine Graham

SHARING

When I consider all the ways that God has blessed me, I naturally want to share my love of life with others. I can do that by sharing the joy and hope that I feel and the vision of peace I hold in mind and prayer.

I share my joy. My happiness is from knowing my oneness with God—spiritual joy that motivates me every day. I encourage my loved ones to trust in God to guide them as well, and I watch as the beauty of self-confidence is realized by them.

I share my hope. I give thanks to God for the blessing of loved ones and embrace them in my prayers for wisdom and success.

I share my vision of peace. I can foresee a time when all people will be united in love and faith and living in harmony. With each thought of goodwill toward others, I am sharing my love of life.

I share my love of life with others.

Day 115

The more you praise and celebrate your life,
the more there is in life to celebrate.
—Oprah Winfrey

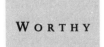

WORTHY

How can I do anything right if I am punishing myself by thinking about what I have done wrong? The quickest way back up from such a downward emotional spiral is to stop giving the energy of my thoughts to what I have done or should have done.

Of course, I admit when I have missed the mark or done less than I am capable of doing, so that I can do better next time. I know that God believes that I can *be* more. When I have been self-critical or others have criticized me, God encourages me by calling me higher: "You are My beloved, and I have created you to love and be loved."

Out of my gratitude to God, I move higher. God loves me; what greater confirmation could I have that I am worthy of love?

God loves me; I am God's creation and worthy of love.

DAILY WORD FOR FAMILIES

Day 116

—◆—

The kindness and affection from the public have carried me through some of the most difficult periods, and always your love and affection have eased the journey.
—Diana, Princess of Wales

SPIRITUAL NATURE

While the eyes have been called the windows to the soul, I know that only God can truly see into the depths of my being. The image I see in a mirror is only a reflection of my physical self.

So in all circumstances, I do my best to reflect my inner spiritual nature out into my world. I remember that the spirit of God resides at the core of each person. As I meet and interact with others, I look beyond the physical to see the divine that is within them also.

I may not agree with what others do or say; however, I find no fulfillment in judging them or their actions. Rather, I bless them on their life journeys and pray that they answer the call of Spirit—an invitation to be divinely guided along their way.

I reflect my spiritual nature out into the world.

Day 117

—◆—

To live, to breathe, to think, to love—these are miracles enough to justify our existence.
—Martha Smock

MIRACLE OF LIFE How wonderful it is to be alive! How awe-inspiring is this magnificent body in which I live and move about! How faithfully it serves me!

Each breath I take fills my lungs with nourishing oxygen and reminds me of the spiritually enriching ideas that are continually flowing into my mind. *Yes,* each breath is a reminder of the miraculous workings of Spirit in caring about me and for me.

Every moment of life is a miracle—a miracle of incredible order and power! With every movement and function of my body, I am reminded that I am a living, breathing miracle of life.

What wonders—what miracles—God has created with all the forms of life on planet Earth!

Life is a miracle!

Day 118

— ◆ —

What was most significant about the lunar voyage was not that men set foot on the moon, but that they set eye on the Earth.—Norman Cousins

ANSWER THE CALL Every day the spirit of God within me gives me a wake-up call to life. So I listen. I answer the call by living my life with enthusiasm, joy, and purpose.

I truly want to be an expression of God's love to others, and this desire leads me to answer the call of God, the call to be loving.

I answer the call to prayer and dedicate some of my time every day to the sacred activity of prayer. This is a communion of the soul that awakens me to my own spirituality.

Ready to answer the call of Spirit, I am awake— spiritually, physically, and mentally.

I answer the call to life joyfully!

Day 119

—◆—

Friendships multiply joys
and divide griefs.
—H. G. Bohn

WELCOME,
FRIEND!
Friendship is a connection of love and acceptance that enriches each friend. I believe that *being* a friend brings as much joy into my life as *having* a friend does.

As a friend, I give from the love of God within me. I love for the sheer joy of loving. Love flowing through me and out to others nourishes every cell of my body.

Every time I welcome friends into my life, I also welcome opportunities to be God's love in action. I see past the personalities of others to the truth that is unique to us all: We are God's individual creations, united in a divine family.

Being a friend at all times is being love at all times. Being a friend is such a joy! What a joy having friends is! I never want to be anything less than a friend. I welcome the world of people as my friends.

Oh, how good it feels to be a friend to all the world!

Day 120

—◆—

Circle of Love

We may often think about how much better life would be if only others were kinder or more considerate. Our cry may be, "How can I change the people I live with and work with!"

Yet the truth is that the desire to change must come from each person. Living a spiritually enriched life sparks the desire in all of us to do better and to be kinder. Relying on the spirit of God within for guidance and strength, life and health is a dedication to living a spiritually enriched life.

We are each important links in a circle of love that is the family of God. Sometimes just being that strong, faith-filled link is the most important thing we can do to help others.

We hold them in prayer and help steady them along the way. By knowing that it is the love of God that links us, we are naturally loving and considerate and fulfilled in our relationships.

The soul gives unity to what
it looks at with love.
—Thomas Carlyle

The Miracle of Discovery
by Naomi Judd

I n my twenties, I was living off Sunset Strip in Hollywood. Divorced and struggling to raise two babies, Wynonna and Ashley, I had no job skills and was working for minimum wage. I found myself in an abusive relationship—a man I thought was the boy-next-door type turned out to be an ex-con who did heroin and beat me. I had no car and no friends, but worst of all I was also lacking self-esteem. Low self-worth or self-respect leads to trouble, because people attract whatever they feel worthy of.

One day, I was looking in the mirror and trying to put on enough pancake makeup to cover a big black shiner. That mirror became a mirror of truth for me, because I realized that my life was as grotesque as the battered face staring back at me.

In that moment, I had a life-changing epiphany. I understood that the deepest source of my identity is God, and as a child of the most high God, I was special. Anything was possible for me! I had been so lonely, desperate, trapped, and out of control, but now I realized I had *everything* because I knew God.

I started questioning everything in my life. I would ask, "Is this what God intends for me to do?" Once I started holding everything up to the light of God's truth, I made some life-changing choices: I moved back to my home in Kentucky and enrolled in nursing school. I realized that the relationship I wanted was with a person who held the same value system and beliefs that I held.

By living on a mountaintop in Kentucky without a TV or telephone, Wynonna and Ashley were able to discover their own talents. Wynonna's discovery was music—singing and playing her guitar by the hour. Ashley discovered books, which planted a seed for her development and a fascination with literature and acting.

During that time, I realized how much fun taking a risk could be. We took a leap of faith and moved to Nashville, Tennessee. I had $200 in my cheap pocketbook and an old beat-up car that Ashley and Wynonna called the hunk of junk. Sometime later, Wynonna and I signed a contract with RCA records after a rare live audition.

The Judds reached success in the country music field, and I was literally on top of the world until that fateful day I was diagnosed with a life-threatening liver illness—hepatitis C. That's when I went on a voyage of self-discovery, on a journey to wholeness. I discovered that peace of mind is more than the absence of a conflict or disease. I found peace of mind knowing that I was a spiritual being going through a human experience. It was not what was happening to me in life, it was what I did with it.

I learned from brilliant medical experts and studied the relationship between spirit, mind, and body. I was so encouraged by the hard empirical data there was in support of prayer and positive beliefs. I had hope—a gift from God that kept me from sinking down into fear and propelled me toward healing.

And I'm a documented miracle—I'm cured! In 1998, I testified at a congressional luncheon on Capitol Hill where I was surrounded by the leading liver specialists in the country. This was an opportunity for me to tell people that there *is* hope, that faith is a more powerful medicine than pills or surgery.

Observation is the key to transformation. We transform our lives when we start putting together the emotional jigsaw puzzle of our lives by first being an observer. I'm such a proponent of people having quiet time—a time of turning off the media and taking charge of their lives so that they can become observers in life, not just robots.

I've learned the practice of mindfulness and being fully present in the moment. I call it living in the present, in God's presence. What is most important of all is holding on to our faith and hope by knowing that we are children of God.

Day 121

— ◆ —

God wants all of us to manifest His life, His radiant,
glowing health, His joy—in fact, all that He is. The creator
is now breathing His purifying, vitalizing, cleansing
breath of life into each cell and fiber of your body.
—Myrtle Fillmore

VITALLY ALIVE If I am feeling less than well and whole, I remember that I am so much more than what a temporary physical condition may be indicating.

I am a divine creation! The truth of my being does not lie in how my body looks or acts; this truth is within my soul. I am a divine being, eternally alive and well with the life of God.

The life of God regenerates my mind and heals my body. As I rest quietly in an awareness of God's presence within me, I feel new energy rising within.

Every thought of healing is a prayer. So I keep my mind centered on the presence of God. God's presence enlivens me. Thought by thought, prayer by prayer, I become stronger and healthier.

I am vitally alive in mind, body, and spirit.

Day 122

—◆—

Your children need your presence
more than your presents.
—Jesse Jackson

C o u n t
O n G o d

In my prayers for others, I send them a silent blessing that lets them know I am always on their side.

"Beloved, wherever you go and whatever you do, I am right there with you in thought and prayer. My support is always with you as you continue on.

"God is giving you all the strength you will ever need. If you feel lost or confused, know that you are not alone, for I am praying with you and for you. Trust in God, and God will show you how to overcome any obstacle in your way.

"Through the darkest of nights, God is the light that guides you safely home. On the brightest of days, God provides you with shade so that you may rest. God is your peace, beloved, and in that loving, peace-filled presence, you are whole and free."

I count on God's loving presence to soothe
and comfort me and my loved ones.

Day 123

—◆—

Are we willing to give up some things we like to do,
to move on to those things we must do?
—Satenig St. Marie

WILLING HEART

I try never to underestimate the importance of my *willingness* to do something in order to be successful in *accomplishing* it. A willing heart has a direct connection to the sacred soul, and my willing heart responds to my sacred soul. I am ready to act on the guidance I receive from God.

Sometimes divine guidance is a gentle urging that prompts me to say or do something. I may not fully know until *after* I have done it or said it that it was a divine idea. Nevertheless, because I am ready and willing to follow God, my responses can be instantaneous. I feel no reluctance in making a decision or in choosing between alternatives.

Oh, how good I feel in having a willing heart! It is my choice to follow God.

God, with all the willingness
of my heart, I follow You.

Day 124

—◆—

The most excellent and divine counsel, the best and most profitable advertisement of all others . . . is to study and learn how to know ourselves. This is the foundation of wisdom and the highway to whatever is good.
—*Pierre Charron*

GROWTH

I am learning that the people I get along with the *least* are the ones who teach me the *most* about relationships and how to achieve harmony in them. My guess is that because they get my attention, the experiences that cause me discomfort are often the ones that propel me forward in growth.

However, there is no rule that says I have to go through painful experiences in order to learn. When I am faced with challenges, it is up to me to decide how I will react. I can let events overwhelm me, or I can welcome them as golden opportunities that will lead me forward.

My choice is to recognize challenges as times in which I learn more about myself and about the blessings of each new day.

I welcome the growth that each person and experience offer me.

Day 125

—◆—

Our real work is prayer. What good is the cold iron
of our frantic little efforts unless first we heat it
in the furnace of our prayer? Only heat will diffuse heat.
—*Mother Maribel*

TALKING WITH GOD

I may wonder when is the best time to pray for help and inspiration. Putting aside all questioning, I know that *any* time is the best time. God is with me all the time, ready to listen and guide me through the ups and downs of life.

I do not have to wait for a formal time of prayer to give God the concerns of my heart. I can talk to God anytime, for God is a loving presence that is with me through every moment of the day and night.

The thoughts I think and the actions I take speak of my beliefs. Each encouraging word is a statement to God about how much I value life and how grateful I am for life. My loving actions are gentle reminders of God's comforting presence. My conversations with God bless me and help me to bless others.

Each prayer is a conversation
with God that blesses me.

Day 126

—◆—

*The most beautiful thing we can experience is the
mysterious. It is the source of all true art and all science.
He to whom this emotion is a stranger, who can no longer
pause to wonder and stand rapt in awe, is as good
as dead: His eyes are closed.—Albert Einstein*

SURRENDER The greatest boost to my own peace of mind comes as I surrender all problems and concerns to God. With one simple affirmation, *I trust You, God,* I open my life to the divine. I allow the power of God to flow through my words and actions and out into every situation.

When I consider the magnificence that God has created and allowed me to be a part of, I am filled with reverence. I give thanks for the divine order that is consistently maintained in my life and throughout the entire planet.

Trusting God is inviting the Holy Presence to move in my life. I no longer feel an urgency about any situation because I surrender to God and know that God is in complete charge.

I trust You, God.

Day 127

---◆---

*And now that I don't want to own anything anymore
and am free, now I suddenly own everything, now
my inner riches are immeasurable.*
—Etty Hillesum

**ONE
WITH
GOD**

In silent communion with God, I
know with a certainty that is beyond
mere human knowing that God and I
are one. We are all one—one with God
and one with each other. This oneness sets me free.

I am free with the freedom of Spirit! The Spirit of life
within me is my heritage of freedom. I am a beloved
child of God. As a beloved child, I am made in the
image of God; I am spiritually free and without
limitation.

As I embrace the idea of my spiritual freedom and
then live from that belief every day, I will help
transform my life. This transformation happens the
world over as person by person recognizes the
sacredness of all life.

**I am one with God, and this oneness
of spirit sets me free.**

Day 128

— ◆ —

Hide not your talents,
they for use were made.
What's a sundial in the shade?
—Benjamin Franklin

T R U E
S E L F

Sometimes it is while I am going through the bleakest of circumstances that I discover my true potential. Then, without hesitation, I rely on divine ideas and give them expression through my actions.

All that I am capable of achieving is already within me. At the right time and place, I call upon these divine qualities. I test my spiritual wings and see how high I am capable of soaring.

When those moments come, I can relax, knowing that I am fulfilling a divine appointment. In the face of any challenge, I draw on the strength of God within me.

Discovering my true self is uncovering my spiritual identity. Then it is up to me to be true to myself in all that I do.

My true self is a divine being, expressing
divine ideas in all that I do.

Day 129

— ♦ —

*Resolve to keep happy, and your joy shall form
an invincible host against difficulty.*
—Helen Keller

AWAKEN TO GOD Embraced by the radiance of this new day, I am filled with the joy of discovery! What I have discovered is this: An awareness of God's presence and love is reborn in me today!

With a fresh, new outlook, I behold the glory of God everywhere. The presence of God within me shines out from me as pure love. Each loving word I speak serves as a reminder of divine light that shines within me and within all people.

God and I are one. One with God, I share a unity of spirit with everyone—the people I know and those I have yet to know. As God's family, we are forever united in a spirit of love and peace.

Yes, an awareness of God's presence and love is reborn in me, and I awaken to God's promise: "I am with you." (Genesis 28:15)

**An awareness of God's presence and love
is reborn in me today!**

Day 130

———◆———

It is like a mustard seed, which, when sown upon the ground, is the smallest of all the seeds on earth; yet when it is sown it grows up and becomes the greatest of all shrubs, and puts forth large branches, so that the birds of the air can make nests in its shade.—Mark 4:31–32

KINGDOM OF GOD No amount of faith is too small—not even faith that is the size of a tiny mustard seed. The mustard seed may be small, but it has the potential to grow and become a safe shelter in which birds can make a home.

So if, at times, I feel as if my faith is too small, I remember the mustard seed: It grows surely and steadily until its roots are planted firmly in the soil. With faith such as this, I can withstand any challenge, and nothing is impossible for me!

Just as the mustard plant provides shelter for birds that nest in its branches, God is my shelter. With God, I know that all things truly are possible.

My faith in God is constant and growing.

DAILY WORD FOR FAMILIES

Day 131

---◆---

I think the one lesson I have learned
is that there is no substitute for paying attention.
—Diane Sawyer

LISTEN TO GOD If I were to ask a question that I genuinely wanted to know the answer to, I would naturally listen and give my full attention to that answer. So when I am praying for God's guidance and direction, I will give no less than 100 percent of my attention to the divine answer I receive.

It just might be that the answer I receive is not the one I am expecting or even one that I want to hear. But I will be ready as I let my faith guide me. I listen with my heart as well as my mind, and I trust God. I know without a doubt that God's wisdom is far greater than my own.

God may speak to me as a whisper, an idea, or a feeling, so I listen with my whole being.

God speaks to me, and I listen.

Day 132

◆

Good timber does not grow with ease.
The stronger the wind, the stronger the trees.
—Williard Marriott

GOD CARES

On a hot day, a leafy, green tree offers shelter from the sun. However, during a lightning storm, good judgment tells me that seeking shelter under the tree might prove to be harmful. It is still the same tree, but I must consider the conditions around it in order to make a decision.

I know that I will make right decisions when I listen to the guidance I receive from God. Knowing that God is always caring for me and is giving me a sense of good judgment, I experience true peace and security.

At all times, God is with me. As I rely on divine guidance and use good judgment, I understand that God cares about me. In any situation and at any time during the day or night, I am in God's care.

Wherever I am, I am in the loving care of God.

Day 133

---◆---

I say that if each person in this world will simply take a small piece of this huge thing, this tablecloth, bedspread, whatever, and work it regardless of the color of the yarn, we will have harmony on this planet.—Cicely Tyson

INSTRUMENT OF PEACE To live in peace and harmony is my hope and the hope of people throughout the world. As I join with others in prayer for this common cause, a spiritual renaissance of global peace is taking place within me and within all the citizens of Earth.

My dream can and will become a reality as I continue to follow the guidance of God. I *can* make a difference, so daily I pray: "Dear God, use me as an instrument of peace. Speak through me with words of faith, hope, and love. Guide my actions and help me to be kind and loving toward others."

With love in my heart and peace in my mind, I am an instrument of harmony.

I am an instrument of peace and harmony.

Day 134

— ◆ —

The foolish man seeks happiness in the distance;
the wise grows it under his feet.
—James Oppenheim

SPRINGTIME OF THE SOUL

There is a way to put joy into a seemingly joyless life and to put even more joy into a life of joy. Every moment I spend in an awareness of God, I reach down within me to a reservoir of spiritual gladness.

Seeing the once dormant trees of winter bursting forth with beautiful, fragrant blossoms reminds me that the spirit of God is within me and ready to burst forth in a springtime of my soul. Yet this will happen only to the degree that I let it happen.

So with my whole being, I invite joy to spread throughout my body in waves of delight and then flow out into my life. God is my joy within the happy times and in spite of any sad times.

The joy in every moment is God.

I enter into a springtime of the soul,
knowing that God is my joy.

Day 135

— ♦ —

Life is not easy for any of us. But it is a continual challenge, and it is up to us to be cheerful and to be strong, so that those who depend on us may draw strength from our example.—Rose Kennedy

WHY ME?

In a difficult situation, it would be easy for me to question, "Why me?" However, God has faith in my ability to surmount any challenge, and the answer from God will always be: "I will not let you go through this alone."

Every experience, whether easy or difficult, is an opportunity to learn more about God and how God expresses wisdom through me. So rather than thinking about the negative in a situation, I think about the divine possibilities. I thank God for the experiences I have had and will have in the future.

The most important relationship in my life is my relationship with God, and I know that God would never punish me. So I keep the lines of communication open. At the slightest feeling of doubt, I remind myself that God is with me.

I never go through anything without God.

Day 136

---◆---

For the Children

Hello God,

Are You there, God? I've been thinking about You a lot today because I've been kind of scared. Growing up is hard sometimes.

There are so many new things to learn and do, and I almost feel like I am never going to get anything right. But Mommy says that is because I'm growing up and finding out what I am really good at.

I'm glad You are on my side, God, and I'm glad that You gave me such special people to help me when I need it. When Mommy or Daddy gives me a hug, I imagine that You are hugging me, too, and I feel special inside.

Just talking to You makes me feel special, like I am somebody important. I feel much better now that we have had this talk. So are You ready to go play?

Day 137

— ◆ —

*Nothing contributes so much to tranquilize the mind
as a steady purpose—a point on which the soul
may fix its intellectual eye.*
—Mary Wollstonecraft Shelley

SERENITY As I look at the majesty of the world around me, I am awestruck by all that God has created. When I understand that the same divine source that created this world also created me, I am filled with peace and a sense of purpose.

My true peace of mind comes from knowing the love of God and then letting divine love nurture me. There is a serenity growing within me that contributes to my being confident at all times. Whatever this day presents, I know that God loves me and will guide me through it all.

Because the peace of God is within me, I remain calm and compassionate in my interactions with others.

**Strengthened by the love of God, I am calm
and peaceful at all times.**

Day 138

—◆—

I am longing to see you so that I may share
with you some spiritual gift to strengthen you.
—Romans 1:11

SHARING BRINGS PROSPERITY Many of my first lessons in life were about sharing—my toys and my treats, my time and my love. And the lessons in sharing have continued throughout my lifetime.

The more I experience, the more I understand that sharing is a part of God's plan of prosperity for me. So I practice sharing by showing my appreciation. Today I consider how beautiful trees and other plants are. I also appreciate that they are a life support for me as they replenish the supply of oxygen in the air I breathe.

How prosperous and blessed I feel as I see new and old trees growing. How comforting it is to stroke the grass and know that each blade is not only sharing a home—planet Earth—but also sharing life with me.

My prosperity increases as I share whatever has blessed me.

Day 139

*It is the creative potential itself in human beings
that is the image of God.*
—Mary Daly

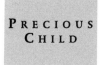

**PRECIOUS
CHILD**

I am God's beloved child and precious in God's sight. I honor God by being the magnificent creation that fulfills a divine plan.

God loves me and cherishes me, offering me support and guidance so that whenever I need them, they are mine. God is here for me always.

I am a priceless creation. No other person can give to the world what is mine alone to give. I have innate qualities that contribute to my being the vibrant individual that I am capable of being.

I am a direct expression of God's wishes for me. Yet even in this moment, I am becoming more—more loving, more kind, more of all that the potential that is within me cheers me on to be.

I am God's precious child.

Day 140

—◆—

All there is responds to a word of praise. God responds.
We respond. Everything responds. The whole world
sparkles, quivers, comes alive.
—James Dillet Freeman

APPRECIATION

Dear God, at every crossroad in my life, You have been there to guide me, to encourage me, to strengthen my resolve. And I show my appreciation for all that You do by being the best person I can be— all according to Your design.

Thank You, God, for each day's blessings and for Your constant, active presence in my life. My appreciation for all that You have done and will do for me includes the blessing of family and friends.

In every moment, I want to live fully in the light of Your love. When I am able to do this, I feel a direct connection with Your wisdom and serenity. My words may not seem to adequately express my appreciation, God, but I believe my faith speaks volumes of thanksgiving to You.

Dear God, I appreciate You.

Day 141

◆

*Spiritual love is a position of standing with one hand
extended into the universe and one hand extended into the
world, letting ourselves be a conduit for passing energy.*
—*Christina Baldwin*

REACH OUT IN PRAYER
I call upon God in prayers for myself
and for my loved ones. With an
awareness of God, I am also aware
that God's spirit within me and within
those for whom I pray unites us.

For the family members I am with daily and for those
whom I am with only on special occasions, I reach out
in prayer with love and support. I infuse every prayer
for them and every thought of them with love and
appreciation.

In prayer, God reminds me that my loved ones
already have the wisdom and health within them that I
am affirming for them. As they call upon God in prayer,
they unlock their own treasure chests of strength and
wisdom, peace and love. Together, we pray through
any challenge.

I reach out in prayer with love and support.

Day 142

——◆——

You can't have a better tomorrow if you are thinking about yesterday all the time.
—Charles F. Kettering

DIVINE TIMING

Some days, I am better at coping with challenges than on other days. Other times, I may feel as if I am at the end of my patience and strength. However, I follow the suggestion of this adage: "When you come to the end of your rope, tie a knot and hang on."

There is humor in this statement, but also some sound advice. What I hang on to in any time of challenge or crisis is my faith in God. There is always a divine plan at work, so I don't give up hope or give in to fear.

In the next few moments or days, solutions will appear that I had not even considered. I am peaceful as I wait for the divine timing of the resolution to any situation. I immerse myself in prayer, knowing that God is bringing about a divine plan.

Knowing that there is divine timing in all matters, I am inspired.

Day 143

---◆---

My only advice is to stay aware, listen carefully,
and yell for help if you need it.
—Judy Blume

GUIDANCE When I need help, I may turn to trusted friends and family members for advice. Yet all the advice in the world will not help unless it offers me some insight into making a decision about the best action for me to take.

When I ask God for help, I have the answer that is right for me and my situation. God does not make a problem magically go away. Rather, God gives me the ideas I need to make the decisions that are right for me.

In the silence of prayer, God brings great possibilities to my attention. As I listen, my thoughts reach new levels of understanding. I begin to see ways of doing things that I never before thought possible. When the guidance comes, I know that surely this is the answer for which I have been looking!

God gives me guidance that blesses me.

Day 144

—◆—

The true measure of a man is how he treats someone
who can do him absolutely no good.
—Ann Landers

MY PROMISE

I am making a promise today—a sacred declaration born of faith in and reverence for God. This promise rises from my soul and is made with enthusiasm: "Dear God, I love You. With all my heart and soul, I promise to honor You by having reverence for all life. I will do my best to love as You love—unconditionally. You never have condemned or abandoned me for making a mistake, so I try never to pass judgment on others or lose sight of them as important to Your grand design of things.

"God, my desire is to live as pure love, as a being of light and wisdom in the world. I will do everything I know to do to ensure that no person ever leaves my presence without having felt the warmth of my friendship and acceptance."

My sacred promise is to honor God
by honoring all life.

Day 145

—◆—

Without wonder and insight, acting is just a trade.
With it, it becomes creation.
—Bette Davis

SENSE OF WONDER Often, the surprises in my life—the unexpected blessings—bring me a greater understanding of the divine mystery that God is.

A sense of wonder comes over me as I experience the presence of God. Such an experience may come from a feeling of awe radiating within me. Then I know without a doubt that I am in the presence of God.

Somehow, the invisible Presence takes on visibility: The tender look in the eyes of a loved one, the smile beaming from a friend, the love wagging a dog's tail—all are reminders that I am loved and accepted just as I am.

I give thanks for and accept the wonder that God is always holding out to me.

I accept the wonder of God, and blessing after blessing enriches me.

Day 146

—◆—

One ought, every day at least, to hear a little song,
read a good poem, see a fine picture, and, if it
were possible, to speak a few reasonable words.
—Johann Wolfgang von Goethe

WORDS OF LIFE
Whether I realize it or not, everything I say or even think is heard by one of the largest audiences in the world—an audience of more than 75 trillion.

It's true: God has created me with life and intelligence in every cell of my body, and this huge audience of cells responds to what I think and say. So the messages I give my cells are ones that proclaim life and health and renewal.

I speak words of life, and my body responds with an energy that enlivens every organ and muscle. I speak words of health and renewal, and the response within me is healing.

Yes, there is an audience listening to me—an audience that responds to my positive words with renewed life and healing.

My body responds with healing
to my life-affirming words.

Day 147

—◆—

*The ultimate goal should be doing
your best and enjoying it.*
—Peggy Fleming

**BE
THE
BEST**

All parents want what is best for their children. Through loving words and actions, mothers and fathers gently nurture and encourage their children to grow at a pace that is appropriate for their individual development.

God gently guides me through the experiences that will take me to the mountaintop of my growth and development. Yet there will also be times when I feel as if I am venturing out alone. Then I know that, like a child, I need only call out and my loving Parent will respond. This response is divine grace, the love of God in action.

Through grace I have the assurance that God is always ready to help me be my best whether I ask for help or not. I have faith that God's loving presence will be with me always.

**Thank You, God, for grace—Your love helping me
to be my best.**

Day 148

—◆—

*The world is full of magical things patiently
waiting for our wits to grow sharper.*
—*Bertrand Russell*

**DIVINE
FLOW**

I know there is a divine order always active in the universe, but do I also know that divine order is a constant in my life?

I do when I stop relying on situations and circumstances for my hope. I do when I take a deep breath, become still, and draw on inner wisdom for my understanding—all of which open a whole new world of order to me.

I begin to think and speak and act from the presence of God within me. Life takes on new purpose and meaning—as if I have taken a step back and seen the whole panoramic view of life and how I fit into the order of it all. I have found my way. I no longer struggle, for I am caught up in the gentle, constant flow of divine order.

I am living in the flow of divine order.

Day 149

—◆—

GOD IS WITH ME

Whenever there is a change in my regular routine, or I must let go of what is familiar and comfortable for me, I may feel some anxiety.

Yet no matter what that change may be, whether it involves moving to a new home or school, starting a new relationship, or changing a career, I can do it. I relax and know that change is a part of life. I also know that there will always be one constant in my life, and God is the one.

Always available to listen and comfort me, God loves and supports me through every change. If I am moving or traveling, I do it knowing that I can never journey outside God's care. If I am starting a new relationship or job or school, I do so knowing that God is guiding my way. Through any experience, I am strengthened by knowing that God is with me.

God is with me—loving and caring for me.

Day 150

---◆---

Circle of Love

Each day, I am becoming more aware of the beauty within every member of my family of love—a family created by God to help each other and support each other through every moment of life.

I thank God every day for my wonderful family—loving individuals who welcome me with love and acceptance.

No matter how unique the members of my family may be, I recognize within each of them the spark of divinity that gives us all life—a spark that unites us together in harmony and love.

How far you go in life depends on you being tender with the young, compassionate with the aged, sympathetic with the striving, and tolerant of the weak and the strong. Because someday in life, you will have been all of these.
—George Washington Carver

THE GOLDEN TREASURE OF "TWO GUNS"

BY RICHARD JAFOLLA

Two Guns—T.G. to his friends—was always different from his siblings. Although they all were born and raised in the most dangerous part of the city, T.G. was the only one who didn't go to college. He was too busy making money. In fact, he began carrying two guns to protect himself and his money when he was only 16. By the time T.G. was 18, he was one of the most successful drug dealers in the area. And when he turned 25, he was a local legend. Many who are heavily involved in the drug scene die violent deaths, but T.G. was one of the lucky ones—he was sent to jail on his 33rd birthday.

I met T.G. at a drug treatment center where I was his counselor. T.G. entered treatment under court order, and he was angry, sullen, and not very cooperative. High on drugs for much of his life, he never learned the social skills he needed to interact in a normal fashion with those around him.

Accustomed to being his own boss, T.G. was not ready to tackle the hard work of recovery. Instead, he devoted his energies to being stubborn and mean. But T.G. possessed a golden treasure. He had what so many don't have—a loving family. These faithful souls had been there for him during his worst times, and they fully supported him now. One unforgettable Family Day during T.G.'s treatment seared the importance of family into the hearts of everyone present. This was the day T.G. died and Leonard was reborn.

On Family Day, family members of clients in treatment are encouraged to visit their loved ones to show their support. T.G.'s mother was the only member of his immediate family who was able to attend that day.

The meeting began routinely. As moderator, I asked each person to say a few words about why they were there. The first client told a bit about herself, what she hoped to accomplish, and then introduced her parents and children. And so it went for the next 10 minutes—everyone giving superficial comments with no one willing to share his or her feelings.

Then it was T.G.'s mother's turn. She was a soft-spoken woman with the humble elegance of one who has accepted what life has given her and is determined to make the best of it. She quietly spoke her name and said she was there to support her son in his recovery from drug addiction.

T.G. was next. I expected him to give a terse or angry comment, but slowly and haltingly he began his story: "My name is T.G., and I am a drug addict." He went on to say that he had been using and selling drugs since he was 13. He recounted how violent his life had been and how he had wanted to "stop the pain of drugging" for many years but did not know how to "get off the roller coaster." He said that the two weeks he had been in treatment had given him a chance to think about how he had hurt so many people—especially his family. He admitted that he had fought cooperation but that under the quiet encouragement of his family—especially his mother—he had had a change of heart.

"In all those years of drinking and drugging," he confessed, "I always felt the love of my family. They never gave up on me. No matter what I was going through, I knew they loved me. I knew they never approved of what I was doing, and there were many times, when I was high, that they would not even let me into their homes. I thought I hated them when they did that, and I would scream and curse at them. But a few times I heard them crying, and I know now what pain they must have been in."

Struggling to control his quivering voice, he said, "My mother was my very special angel. Mama, I want to say in front of all these people that I am so sorry for what I did to hurt you. I love you, Mama."

With those words the dam broke. All the love hidden in T.G.'s soul, all the love locked up in his heart for two decades, exploded out of him. With one arm around his mother's neck, he began sobbing uncontrollably. His mother tenderly stroked his head while rocking him, repeating over and over again, "It's all right, Leonard. It's all right, baby." Except for Leonard and his Mama, the people sat in utter stillness. Tears flowed down the cheeks of all who had witnessed this heart-wrenching scene and its powerful demonstration of one family's love.

Leonard finished rehabilitation and is clean to this day. He is still involved in the world of drugs, but in a different way—he started a half-way house for recovering drug addicts. He is very involved with each person who stays there because he wants drug addicts to know that someone cares about them—just like his family cared about him. "If it weren't for my family, I would be dead. No matter what I did or how much trouble I was in, I knew that there were people who really cared about me and loved me. It made all the difference."

Day 151

—◆—

We first must think "I can," then behave
appropriately along that line of thought.
—Marsha Sinetar

I CAN!
Throughout life, I have had experiences that challenged me, and it was in those situations that I found the strength I needed to say, "I can!" *I can* face each new day with confidence, and *I can* do those things that are mine to do. I have faith in God and faith in myself.

So no matter what has happened in the past, today can be a new start for me. I claim new life in my body through the spirit of God within me. I claim a new way of living through the wisdom of God being expressed by me. *I can!*

Today and every day is a new start in life for me. It is up to me to accept it, and I take responsibility for that now. There is a new me and a new way of life emerging for me. I will not repeat the mistakes of the past because I am starting over in a new life. *I can!*

I claim the new start in life
that is being offered to me now.

DAILY WORD FOR FAMILIES

Day 152

—◆—

*Joy increases as you give it and diminishes as you
try to keep it for yourself. In giving it, you will accumulate
a deposit of joy greater than you ever believed possible.*
—*Norman Vincent Peale*

**CHEERFUL
HEART**

The natural response of a cheerful
heart is to be drawn to a person who
has a happy smile, a positive attitude, a
face that shines with joy. And when
my outlook is positive and I feel happy, my life
continues to host uplifting experiences.

God has created me and everyone else to be happy,
to find joy and laughter in all the different stages and
experiences of life. So when I sense this joy in others, I
am drawn to that expression of God's joy in them.

I feel so good as I release the joy of God from within!
What better proof could I have of God's eternal, loving
presence within me and within all people?

**My cheerful heart uplifts me and brings joy
to those around me.**

Day 153

---◆---

I expect to pass through this world but once. Any good, therefore, that I can do, or any kindness or abilities that I can show to any fellow creature, let me do it now.
—*William Penn*

THE FULLNESS OF GOD

My physical characteristics and other features create an image that identifies me as a person. However, my essence—that which enlivens and nurtures me—is within. This "me" is a spiritual being, for the spirit of God lives within me.

I now begin to live my life from the inside out, from the spirit of God within me to the world of God around me. My spiritual nature is a blessing I bring to my relationships, my work, and my life.

The joy in my voice and the warmth of my presence are inspired by the spirit of God. Living life from the inside out is an adventure in living life to the fullest. As I do, I release the fullness of God within me out into the world around me.

I live my life from the spirit of God within me.

Day 154

—◆—

In relation to others, gratitude is good manners;
in relation to ourselves, it is a habit of the heart and
a spiritual discipline.—Daphne Rose Kingman

REBIRTH OF THE HEART

In some areas of the world, there are well-defined seasons during the year. For those areas, spring is a time of rebirth, for these regions that were once barren during winter are now teeming with new life.

In my own life, I can have that springtime experience of rebirth and renewal by awakening my heart again to the glory of God all around me. My heart is alive with the spirit of God! I am inspired by the joy of God and refreshed by the love of God. I am full of gratitude.

There is a rebirth in my heart as I experience a resurgence of faith. The skies are bluer than ever before, the stars twinkle brighter in the evening sky, and the days are filled with endless possibilities.

It is springtime in my heart, and I am alive with life!

Day 155

—◆—

Like an ability or a muscle, hearing
your inner wisdom is strengthened by doing it.
—Robbie Gass

FOCUS

When I am concentrating intensely on a project, a sudden interruption can distract me and cause me to feel confused. I may even forget what I was thinking about or doing. My focus has changed, and I need to make an adjustment in order to have a clear image of what I am doing.

Yet whether I am easily distracted or not, I know that my most important focus is always on God. Nothing else could ever be as important to me as letting God's light shine out from me and into the world.

When I let my inner light shine, no outer distraction can pull me off course. God will lead me over the most difficult of roads and keep me moving steadily forward—all in divine order.

When I keep my attention on God,
my whole life comes into focus.

Day 156

---◆---

*All the time a person is a child, he is both a child
and learning to be a parent. After he becomes a parent,
he becomes predominantly a parent reliving childhood.*
—Benjamin Spock

THE CHILD IN ME
It seems to take no effort at all for a child to be open to discovering the wonder of life. However, retaining this same openness and enthusiasm as an adult is a matter of choice.

Today I make this my choice. I choose to be childlike to the extent that I have a positive, joyful attitude about all matters. I do this by letting the loving spirit of God within me become part of all my activities.

Today I choose to be childlike in my joy. I view the world through eyes filled with wonder and excitement, and I feel a sense of carefree abandon that leads me to incredible discoveries. The joy of expectation lightens my steps and brightens my day.

**I choose to be a child who is open to
the wonder of life.**

Day 157

—◆—

Put these things into practice, devoting yourself to them,
so that all may see your progress. Pay close attention
to yourself and to your teaching.
—1 Timothy 4:15–16

SHOW ME THE WAY I don't give up when a door closes in my life because I know that God will open a window to new opportunities.

So when I come to the end of a relationship or job or way of life, I trust God and let go. I let go and let God open the way to the new blessings that are in store for me.

As I let go and let God, God shows me the way. God gives me the strength and courage I need to take the first step in a new direction or to go back one step, if that is necessary.

I let go and let God. I let go of fears. I let go of any concern I may have about the future. God is in charge, and I know that God is guiding me to the place where I will find the greatest fulfillment and peace.

As I let go and let God, new opportunities
open to me.

Day 158

◆

Without change, something sleeps inside us
and seldom awakens. The sleeper must awaken.
—Frank Herbert

DIVINE PRESENCE Life is not always easy, but God is always with me to help me along the way. I imagine what it was like as a toddler learning how to walk. I must have felt some fear. Yet I let go of my parent's hand in order to experience the freedom of moving about on my own. The powerful spirit of God within me was inspiring me on.

As an adult, I know that letting go of a child, spouse, or parent is never easy. Whenever a temporary separation comes, I may feel a tug on the vital connection that has kept us close. If the separation is more than temporary, I may feel as if it is the hardest thing I have ever done.

But this I know: God is with me so that I and my loved ones will never go through anything alone. We will never be without the love and comfort of God.

Because the divine Presence is with me,
I am never alone.

Day 159

— ♦ —

*The art of peace begins with you. . . . Foster peace in
your own life and then apply the art to all you encounter.*
—Morihei Ueshiba

**UNLOAD
BURDENS**

If I carry a package with me long
enough, I may become so used to it
that I forget to set it down. The same is
true of emotional burdens. Am I
holding on to any unforgiveness from the past? If I am,
I need to unload. I don't want to become so used to
hurt feelings that I do not recognize the damage they
are doing to my peace of mind.

So in prayer I ask God to show me what I cannot
recognize. In the silence, anything that I need to release
is made known to me. I then begin a healing process by
forgiving myself and others. Even if I no longer have
any contact with these people, forgiving them helps to
heal my mind and heart.

I affirm: *Today is a new day. I cannot change the past, but I
can forgive everyone and everything from the past.* Then I
thank God for the peace of mind that flows over me.

**This is a new day and a new chance
for greater peace of mind.**

Day 160

---◆---

Every single one of us can do things that no one else can do—can love things that no one else can love. . . .
We are like violins. We can be used for doorstops, or we can make music.—Barbara Sher

LOVING EMBRACE God, for everyone who cries out in the day or night, let there be caregivers who answer with a soft, assuring word. For everyone who needs attention and care, let there be a warm and responsive person who is willing to be an expression of love to them.

Whether giving a tender touch or a strong embrace, there are people who comfort and nurture children and adults without thought of recognition. What shining examples they are to all humanity! What expressions of Your love they are!

Thank You, God, for creating these instruments of Your love throughout the world. With every caring thought and act, they are fulfilling a sacred commitment to You and to love.

I celebrate all who have been or who are expressions of love to the world.

Day 161

— ◆ —

I was the kind nobody thought could make it. I had a funny Boston accent. I couldn't pronounce my Rs. I wasn't a beauty.—Barbara Walters

AUTHENTIC

I may feel compelled to follow the advice of another, but first I ask myself, "Is this what is best for me?"

Only through remaining true to who I am—a beloved child of God—will I find the fulfillment for which I long. I am a child of the Spirit of life that lives within each and every person, and it is to Spirit within me that I remain true. Then I will remain true to what is right for me.

I know that no one else can live my life for me, because no one else can fulfill the purpose for which God has created me. Every moment of every day, God guides me, and I am determined to stay on course. I know that only God can lead me to the place that is right for me and also inspire me to know when I have arrived there.

I am true to who I am—a beloved child of God.

Day 162

—◆—

Therefore my heart is glad,
and my soul rejoices.
—Psalms 16:9

JOURNEY OF THE SOUL

The very act of seeking God's guidance revitalizes me spiritually. So rather than praying for God to show me the way to change something outside me, I simply pray for God to show me the way to the divine ideas already within me.

Divine guidance takes me on a journey of the soul. I meet with God in a sacred atmosphere where I meld mind and heart with Spirit. Then I move from asking what to do or what changes to make in my life to knowing what is best.

"Yes, God, I know what to do in each moment of decision or crisis. Sometimes, that knowing tells me to do nothing more than believe in You. I know there is nothing more powerful I can do than to believe that You will always show me the way and help me choose between any alternatives."

My belief in God opens me to the guidance of God.

Day 163

— ◆ —

Whether or not we realize it, each of us has within us
the ability to set some kind of example for people.
Knowing this, would you rather be the one known for
being the one who encouraged others, or the one who
inadvertently discouraged those around you?—Josh Hinds

TEACHER

Whether or not my chosen profession is that of a teacher, I find myself in the role of a teacher many times throughout my life.

When I am around children, I am teaching by example, for words and actions carry a great impact. Children tend to be easily influenced by older children and adults, so I do my best to exude the joy I feel in being a participant in life.

If I am teaching others how they might achieve some special skill, I use patience and understanding and I make learning fun and comfortable for all involved. I have confidence as a teacher, because God, the greatest teacher, is constantly pouring out wisdom to me.

I am a teacher by divine example.

Day 164

—◆—

The more balanced our lives,
the more serene we feel.
—*Ann Smith*

SOURCE OF PEACE God, whenever I am tired or lonely, You show me that I have strength and comfort in reserve to call upon.

Whether I have recognized it or not, my life has always been in Your care. Looking back at the times when I have felt lost, I now understand that You were there, gently guiding me all the while.

Every time I have consciously made a choice to release anything to You, I have felt at peace immediately. No challenge has been or will be mine alone to solve. I am an instrument through which You bring about solutions. I listen to Your wisdom and allow myself to be guided in doing whatever I need to do or in saying whatever I need to say.

Thank You, God, for being the voice of reason in my moments of doubt, for calming me in times of crisis, and for loving me through it all.

God, You are my source of peace.

Day 165

—◆—

It never occurs to me that
there are things that I can't do.
—Whoopi Goldberg

UNLIMITED FREEDOM

I may be concerned because I have forgotten something—where my car keys are, the time or place of an appointment, or even someone's name.

There is so much to remember; the one thing I remember *never* to forget is my freedom of spirit—a freedom that is critical in every moment of my life.

Because I remember that I am free—free with the freedom infused in me by the spirit of God—I will never limit myself or what I can accomplish. I will never accept that anyone or anything can keep me from living the freedom that God has given me to live.

The spirit of God lives within me and has set me free. *Yes,* I am free! I am free from all that would keep me from excelling in life, and I am free to be all that celebrates my freedom!

I remember that the spirit of God within me
has set me completely free!

Day 166

◆

For the Children

Hello God,

Sometimes I wonder what I will be when I grow up. Will I look like my mom or dad? Will I go to the same job that they go to? Am I going to do great things? Will I have a family of my own?

Sometimes, God, when I think about all of the things that I will do when I grow up, I get scared. But then, just as fast as I felt afraid, I feel okay again. This must be because You are patting me on the back and telling me everything is going to be okay—right, God?

Now, when I imagine all the things I might be doing, I know You will be doing them with me. Just think, God—I can be anything that I want to be! I can be a firefighter, a school teacher, a doctor—anything! And with You there to help me, I know I won't be scared. I can do it!

Thanks, God, for listening. I'm going to be okay, and I am going to be the best me I can be!

Day 167

—◆—

Nine-tenths of wisdom is appreciation. Go find
somebody's hand and squeeze it while there's time.
—Dale Dauten

JOYFUL
APPRECIATION

God shows me what absolute joy is, and the feeling I receive from it is one that will remain a part of me. Because joy is so much a part of me, I want to share it with my loved ones and with the world.

To be a source of joy requires more from me than just mere words; it takes action on my part as well. Often my actions speak even louder than my words.

So I live my life in joyful appreciation of God's glory. Life may still present many mysteries, but I am secure in my faith. Rather than becoming anxious about what I do not know or understand, I embrace every opportunity to learn. In doing so, I am learning more about myself and using that knowledge in my interactions with others.

I am a joyous person because I have God's joy within me.

I know the joy of God!

DAILY WORD FOR FAMILIES

Day 168

—◆—

One ship drives east and the other drives west
by the selfsame winds that blow.
It's the set of the sails and not the gales
that determines the way they go.—Ella Wheeler Wilcox

SACRED STIRRING The very movement of a thought of God's grace in my mind causes me to relax and breathe easier. Such a sacred stirring prompts my heart to beat in a steady, strong rhythm.

The very movement of the words *God's grace* over my tongue and across my lips calms me. Speaking about the grace of God thrills me because it is a powerful message of hope for me and for all that concerns me.

The grace of God moves throughout my life. Because I am aware of the presence of God's grace, I feel the assurance of God's love for me. Love is so active in me that I bring it to every experience of life.

I give thanks that God loves me and moves through me with the power and beauty of grace.

By the grace of God, the presence of God
is always stirring within me.

Day 169

—◆—

I believe God is managing affairs and that He doesn't need any advice from me. With God in charge, I believe everything will work out for the best in the end. So what is there to worry about?—Henry Ford

KEEP ON

When things get rough—as they sometimes do in life—I may think about giving up on a dream or a goal. From deep within, however, I receive the encouragement to keep on keeping on.

I remember that God is with me, that God is ready to help me through every challenge that may come my way. God loves me and has prepared me for success.

I keep faith in God and commit myself to following the guidance and inspiration that I receive. Then I will begin to see that challenges are opportunities for me to learn more about myself and the true desires of my heart and soul.

I keep on keeping on and discover the joy of living my dreams!

Day 170

—◆—

To love another person
is to help them love God.
—Søren Kierkegaard

BLENDING TOGETHER Each individual wildflower fairly shouts its color, seemingly to get the attention of anyone nearby. Collectively, a field of wildflowers creates a panorama of beauty, a harmonious whole.

This same harmonious coexistence is true for humanity as well. I live in a world that is a diverse and complex composite of textures and tones, beliefs and opinions, experiences and skills. But all people can complement each other by living in harmony and love.

Even the people within a family unit are different, and this can be a positive. While working and living together, one person's calmness and another person's eagerness blend together to create a cohesive team.

As a member of God's family, I live according to a divine plan. I contribute something unique to a harmonious whole.

God's plan is for all to live
and work together in harmony.

Day 171

—◆—

Time is free, but it's priceless. You can't own it, but you can use it. You can't keep it, but you can spend it. Once you've lost it, you can never get it back.—Harvey Mackay

UNFOLDING PLAN

I would never take a long trip without planning it out beforehand. So why *wouldn't* I plan ahead for the most important journey I will make on Earth—the journey of my life?

So I do. I live every moment in the light of God so that I know the way to a happy, healthy future. I am confident, for God is my constant companion. I understand that nothing is left to chance because divine order is at work in my life. I also know that I have a responsibility in letting this order unfold. I play an active role as I listen to God and follow the guidance I receive.

God is my navigator. Each day, I see that God and I are making progress *together.* Understanding, peace, and true joy are with me each moment and are included in my plan for each new day.

**God is my companion in this moment
and in every moment of the future.**

Day 172

—◆—

The point of power is always
in the present.
—Louise L. Hay

SIGNS AND WONDERS

I may not be able to see, hear, touch, smell, or taste divine order, yet I am certain that it exists. I am certain because I sense the effects of it all around me. There are, of course, obvious signs of divine order, such as the sun rising and setting and nature providing for all creatures.

If I look even closer, I will find subtle clues to God's order that may be apparent only to me. Perhaps at a time when I need a boost, a favorite song is played on the radio and brightens my day. Or it could be that at the exact time that I am thinking of someone, that person telephones me. Even going to the store and finding the very item I need on sale is evidence of divine order for me.

Divine order may be apparent or not; it may be noticed by everyone or just by me. No matter what, I know that God's order is active in my life and throughout the world.

Divine order is active in my life now and always.

Day 173

—◆—

You have to accept whatever comes, and the only
important thing is that you meet it with the best
you have to give.—Eleanor Roosevelt

ALL THINGS ARE POSSIBLE God does not put conditions upon the power of faith. So why would I limit my faith by assigning a measure to it or doubting that I have enough?
My faith is in God and in God's goodness in my life.

When appearances suggest that things are not going well because the results I expected to happen are not happening, I remind myself that it is God who is in charge, not me.

My faith is in God and God will prevail. With God, all things truly are possible. I know this; I believe this; I live my life based on this.

Because I place my faith in God, I am opening my life to the desires of my heart and to all blessings.

With faith in God, I open my life to all blessings.

Day 174

—◆—

It is possible to make each year bring with it a lasting gift to add to the fullness of experience, to be treasured up, savored, and remembered.—Grenville Kleiser

SPECIAL THANKS Some of the blessings that make my life so sweet are the special people who share my good times and brighten my days. It is these same people who cheer me on when my enthusiasm seems to wane.

It is to these people—dear ones who are always willing to give comfort and support, often without even being asked—that I express my heartfelt thanks today. I love them, and I appreciate all that they have done to make my life happier and more complete. The sweet memories of these unique individuals will continue to bless me all the days of my life.

Whether they are still an active part of my life or they have gone on to continue their own journeys, they hold a special place in my heart.

I give thanks for you always in my prayers.

Day 175

—◆—

Hope is always available to us. When we feel defeated,
we need only take a deep breath and say, "Yes,"
and hope will reappear.—Monroe Forester

STEPPING-STONES In order to cross the width of a shallow stream, I need to find a path of stepping-stones. Then, step by step, I make progress crossing the water and remain dry as I move along.

In my spiritual journey, God provides me with stepping-stones every day so that I can continue on to each new level of awareness and growth. These stepping-stones are available to me in many forms: love, peace, joy, hope, wisdom.

The love of God lifts me to great heights by allowing me to face any situation with understanding and compassion. The joy and peace of God are other steps in my progress. As I step forth in faith, I do not limit any outcome by my own expectations. I allow the wisdom of God to guide me and to inspire me.

God places stepping-stones before me
on my spiritual journey.

Day 176

—◆—

We are each gifted in a unique and important way.
It is our privilege and our adventure to discover
our own special light.—Mary Dunbar

GOD HAS BLESSED ME
Every day I interact with people, some whom I know and others whom I am just beginning to know. As I live and work and learn with others, I find that being patient helps me in being understanding and kind toward them.

God has blessed me with patience, and yet it is up to me to use it. I use it by turning to God and allowing divine peace and love to infuse my every thought and my every move.

God has blessed me with love, and I remain focused on that love. Before I speak, I think loving thoughts. As I deal with others, I react in positive, thoughtful ways.

God has blessed me. The serenity I feel is a direct result of knowing that I am totally and completely in God's care. This serenity nourishes me so that I remain patient and kind toward myself and others.

God has blessed me with patience and love.

Day 177

♦

There are only two lasting bequests we can hope to give our children. One of these is roots, the other, wings.
—Hodding Carter

LIFE OF GOD

I would give my all for my loved ones to spare them any difficulties or pain. Yet I know that the greatest hope for them is God, not me.

So my prayer for family and friends is that they are open to the life of God living through them. I see them blessed with healing that enhances their health and strength to a greater degree than ever before.

My prayer is that they are open to God thinking through them. Such thoughts bless them and, when acted upon, will bless others. Even in their most alone times, a thought from God, a divine idea, will inspire and revive them.

My prayer is that they are open to God loving through them. In every moment that they give expression to God's love, they will feel loved and loving. The love of God heals and refreshes them now and always.

My prayer for loved ones is that they allow God to live, think, and love through them.

Day 178

—◆—

The concept of total wellness recognizes that our every thought, word, and behavior affects our greater health and well-being. And we, in turn, are affected not only emotionally but also physically and spiritually.
—Greg Anderson

HEALING

Much has been written about the importance of faith. It is true that whatever people believe in, whatever people are receptive to, they are likely to draw to them as an experience.

So if I or someone I love has a healing need, I will believe in healing for us. The picture of us I keep in mind is one in which we are healthy and whole. I do not accept symptoms as permanent conditions. I focus on what I know in my heart is true: God created each and every person to express life and wholeness!

God created us to live in joy, to know the wonder of living each day fully and completely. With faith in God, I am guided to being the whole and holy creation of God I was created to be!

God heals me.

Day 179

— ♦ —

You can complain because roses have thorns,
or you can rejoice because thorns have roses.
—Ziggy

GOD ANSWERS

Although I know every day is a blessing, there may be occasions when I feel sad or afraid or alone. However, when I am aware that God is always with me, I discover new courage and new joy. Yes, God loves me and is ready to help me.

So if ever I experience what seems to be a loss or a setback or the unexpected, the best thing I can do for my own peace of mind is to let go of worry and let God embrace me with the comfort I need.

Whenever I call out to God, God answers, soothing me to the depths of my soul and filling me with peace. Gently, lovingly, God assures me that I will be okay, that all will be okay. Embraced by God, I feel comforted, at peace, and ready for a new day.

God comforts me to the very depths of my soul.

Day 180

———◆———

Circle of Love

Throughout our years we have learned from our experiences. We have added to our knowledge of ourselves and our world. There still may be questions as we continue our spiritual growth, but God will always respond to those questions with pure, unconditional love.

If we are seeking peace and assurance, God will answer. We all seek to attain the common goal of living a life of total love and acceptance, and as we unite in oneness of faith, we are encircled in a divine embrace. We not only feel the love that God is giving to us but also we are able to share that love with others. Love gives us the ability to stop and listen to each other.

We may not physically be able to help every person who lives in the world, but—one by one— we give love and aid to one another. Together we share the message of God's love with others—one step at a time.

It is not the going out of the port, but the coming in, that determines the success of a voyage.
—Henry Ward Beecher

A Bond of Love
by Elaine Meyer

T he chirping was persistent, and within that sound was an appeal for help that I couldn't deny. As I often did after school in my early teens, I had gone for a walk in the woods near my house. And it was there that I heard the pitiful sound of a baby bird coming from somewhere on the ground. Being a nature-lover who lived in the country, I was well-versed in raising and caring for animals, so I went to see if I could help.

In no time at all, I found the baby bird. Looking up into the trees, I did not see a nest from which it could have fallen. What I did find, though, were several cats already on the prowl. I could no longer delay my decision: Scooping up the hatchling, I headed back to my house.

Lola, as I had named her, grew bigger and stronger each day. When I had first stumbled upon her, I was uncertain as to what type of bird she was. But as she grew, the unmistakable markings of a mourning dove became evident—a gentle bird that can fill the morning air with the relaxing sound of cooing.

Lola had also found an avid friend and admirer in my grandmother, who lived next door. Grandma always

DAILY WORD FOR FAMILIES

enjoyed our company, and she never failed to have a piece of apple waiting for Lola to enjoy each day. Grandma and I would talk for hours as we worked in the yard or cleaned the house. Lola was always there with us, cooing her song of happiness.

Too soon, though, it was time for Lola to leave the roost. Her full set of feathers had grown in, and she had become a pro at flying. Although I was happy that she would soon be enjoying her freedom, I had become accustomed to listening to the relaxing sound of her gentle cooing and our daily visits with Grandma.

But I had to let her go. As I placed her on a fencepost outside of Grandma's house, I told her how beautiful she was and how much joy she had brought to me and Grandma with her songs. She seemed to know that it was time to say good-bye, and as she bobbed up and down a few times, she cooed gently. Then, with a gentle flap of her wings, she was gone—flying gracefully into the sky and into the distance until I could see her no more.

When I turned, I saw Grandma watching me with an all-knowing smile on her face. "She'll be back!" she assured me. "It's like raising children—you have to have the courage to let them leave the nest. But if you love them, they will never forget that love, and they will always be a part of your life—both physically and in spirit. You gave one of God's creatures the gift of life and love. You will always get back what you give, and when you give in love, then love will always return to you."

True to Grandma's words, Lola returned. One evening, I heard the distinctive coo I had grown so fond of and discovered Lola sitting on the door handle, looking in the window. And she wasn't alone! Beside her was a male mourning dove, watching me intently as if to ensure Lola's safety.

I quickly ran to Grandma's house to tell her that Lola had come for a visit. Hearing the news, Grandma reached for the customary apple and said, "Slice this up and put it on the porch, and let's see if she comes to visit me."

Sure enough, after I put out the pieces of apple, Lola flew over with her companion. Together they ate the apple. In that moment, a tradition began that spanned many years and many generations of Lola's family. Feeding Lola and her ensuing brood over the next several years became a daily routine and a labor of love for Grandma. Every morning she saw to it that the birds had food and fresh water, and every morning she received beautiful songs of contented cooing.

This routine continued until I, too, was ready to leave my parents' roost. I found an apartment of my own, and just as Grandma had affirmed with Lola, I, too, came back to see her as often as possible. Grandma and I shared many common bonds—Lola, gardening, our spirituality—

and the strongest bond of all—our love for each other.

Grandma passed in the late 1980s, and although she was no longer with us physically, her spirit remained as the traditions of love that she had established continued on. Grandpa continued feeding the doves for many years afterward, seeing that there was always food and water for them to enjoy and listening with pleasure to their songs. The gift of life that I had given Lola so many years ago was coming full circle as the children of Lola's children now gave my grandfather a sense of purpose as he adjusted to life without Grandma. He often remarked how they filled him with peace and brought back wonderful memories of Grandma.

I now have a family of my own, and my grandfather, too, has passed from this world. But the lesson that Grandma and Lola taught me will always be fresh in my mind. When my own daughter has grown and is ready to begin a life on her own, I will have the strength to let her go, for I know that our love is a bond that will always keep us together. The love I give her will continue on in the generations to come.

Day 181

---◆---

What the inner voice says will not
disappoint the hoping soul.
—Johann Friedrich von Schiller

LONGING OF THE SOUL

There is a thirst within me, God, that only You can satisfy. Whenever I retreat from my busy life for just a few moments and let myself be aware of You, I am filled with Your presence. Then I feel a peace that is beyond description.

God, I long for peace. Sometimes, though, I become so busy or so focused on something going on in my life that I forget Your peace is always within me. Yet in just that moment when I become still and open myself to a sacred communion with You, I experience a peace that heals me of all anxiety.

In that peace I concentrate on breathing. As I exhale, I release all concern. I inhale and know that it is Your spirit that fills me, enlivens me, and satisfies the longing of my soul.

**God satisfies the longing of my soul,
and I am at peace.**

Day 182

—◆—

Animals were once, for all of us, teachers. They instructed us in ways of being and perceiving that extended our imaginations, that were models for additional possibilities.
—*Joan McIntyre*

**BLESSING
ANIMALS**

How often do I think about the blessing that animals are in my life and in the world? It is true: God has blessed the world with an abundance of unique and magnificent creatures.

All that God has created sustains a wholeness and balance in nature that benefits us all. I have the opportunity to interact with some of these animals and am especially grateful for pets who offer loving companionship and devoted service.

I also give thanks for the animals that, because of their nature or natural habitat, do not interact with me. I recognize that they, too, are fulfilling their God-created roles in nature. I understand that the world would not be complete without each of God's beloved creations.

I bless and appreciate all God's creatures.

Day 183

— ◆ —

You are the activity of God in expression,
beloved with an everlasting love.
—Eric Butterworth

EXPRESSION OF GOD'S LOVE

There is divine order in the universe that brings peace wherever there is unrest, harmony wherever there seems to be only indifference.

This order blesses all people. Because God is in charge, I experience the peace that is God as I live from the love of God within me.

I am an expression of God's love in my own personal life, so I think loving thoughts and speak kind words. I can always act in harmonious ways and I do, because I know God's love for me and how it feels moving out from me.

I have the capacity to express love continually. As I live from the love of God within me, others respond in harmony. We have unlimited love to share with one another.

Being an expression of God's love, I have
unlimited love to share.

Day 184

$—\blacklozenge—$

Nature has been for me, for as long as I can remember,
a source of solace, inspiration, adventure, and delight;
a home, a teacher, a companion.—Lorraine Anderson

WONDER OF GOD
Every day is a day of new opportunities. As I seek God in all I do, I find that God has prepared blessing upon blessing for me to discover and enjoy.

Seeking God is not something I do only in prayer. God is always with me; so when I look at the world with fresh, new eyes, I will discover that God is everywhere—in the people, events, and the miraculous panorama of life around me.

I discover God's beauty in the radiant glow of the sun as it rises over the horizon. I receive God's unconditional love through loved ones. And I can literally feel God's soothing touch in the warm breeze that gently caresses my face. When I look for God in every experience, I will discover that the wonder and beauty of God are everywhere.

As I seek God in all there is, I discover
a whole new world of blessings.

Day 185

—◆—

The soul is made of love and must ever strive to return to love. . . . By its very nature, it must seek God, who is love.
—Mechthild von Magdeburg

GENTLE TOUCH

If I have been waiting for a booming voice to reveal a decision I need to make, then I could be missing out on divine guidance—as the gentle voice of God within me.

God is all power and all gentleness, too. God lovingly guides me through every circumstance with a divine plan, a blueprint that is absolutely right for me.

I am preparing myself for great and wonderful outcomes when I surrender to God, so I listen to and follow divine guidance. In that surrender, I hear the gentleness of God speaking to me and feel the power of God enlivening me.

How blessed I am in knowing that God is guiding me! The fog of confusion is lifted, and the light of understanding shines brightly within me now.

**I surrender to God, and I am blessed
with divine guidance.**

Day 186

— ◆ —

Gratitude unlocks the fullness of life. . . . It can turn a meal into a feast, a house into a home, a stranger into a friend.
—*Melody Beattie*

JOY OF LIVING

What could be nicer on a warm summer day than being outside and listening to songbirds? Each feathered friend gives its all in filling the air with the sweet music of gratitude. The melodies are joy-filled messages of God's love for all creation.

I, too, feel the joy of God's love. Such joy comes from a satisfaction that I feel in my soul—a peace that comes from knowing the presence of God.

I am filled with the joy of living! With joy in my heart, I can face any change that the future may bring. Whatever the day may hold, I greet it with expectation.

I can bring the joy of God into any situation and help bring about the right outcome every time. By knowing God, I know pure and everlasting joy.

The joy of God fills my heart.

Day 187

—◆—

*Twenty years from now, you will be more disappointed
by the things you didn't do than by the ones you did do.
So throw off the bowlines. Sail away from the safe harbor.
Catch the trade winds in your sails. Explore.
Dream. Discover.—Mark Twain*

**DIVINE
GIFTS**

I am a unique and special creation of
God—created like no other and given
the gifts of special talents and abilities.
My gift may be the ability to make
someone laugh or to be a good listener. I may have the
aptitude for creative thinking or for creative doing—
using my mind and my hands. All that I have been
given I use to express my appreciation of God's grace.

Grace is God's love in action. So when I use my
unique gifts, I am honoring God and helping to bless
family and friends, co-workers and strangers. As I share
who I am, I share an enthusiasm for life, blessing myself
and others through giving expression to God's gifts.

**God's grace expresses itself through me
as I use the gifts God has given me.**

Day 188

— ◆ —

To love is to receive
a glimpse of heaven.
—Karen Sunde

GROUNDED IN LOVE God, You are there in the beginning of my new relationship, so that the other person and I are grounded in love and reverence for all life and for each other.

Each day that we build on that sacred beginning, we are gentle and patient with each other. We understand that we are not dependent on each other for happiness, but that the individual happiness of each of us is enhanced by our unity.

God—whether as a spouse, parent, or friend—You are right there in my longtime relationships and You are renewing them each moment. What a pleasure it is to watch family and friends become more and more the wonders You created them to be! What a pleasure it is to be in partnership with You!

My relationships with others
are grounded in love.

Day 189

— ◆ —

*Is he alone who has courage on his right hand
and faith on his left hand?*
—Charles A. Lindbergh

**S E C U R E
W I T H
G O D**

A feeling of security is important if I am to feel comfortable in my home, at school, at my place of employment, or anywhere else I may be. The more secure I feel physically and emotionally, the easier it is for me to be at ease. I do my best by being myself.

"God, thank You for keeping me safe and secure." Saying this prayer as I start the day and then as I begin each new project, I am filled with a sense of well-being. I know that God loves me and is giving me a fresh, new day to explore and enjoy.

Every moment of every day, I am enfolded in God's loving embrace. I feel safe and secure, because I know that the guidance of God is with me wherever I go. My prayer is that I will listen to and follow God's guidance—always.

God, thank You for keeping me safe and secure.

Day 190

—◆—

An infinite God can give all of Himself to each
of His children . . . as fully as if there were no others.
—*A. W. Tozer*

G O D
I S W I T H
Y O U

Dear God, as much as I want to be
of help to my loved ones, I cannot
always be with them as they go
through both the challenges and the
celebrations of today. But I feel such peace in knowing
that You will be there with each one.

Whether it is their skills or their patience that is being
tested, I know You are unlimited wisdom and
compassion within them. God, I pray that they know
this truth about themselves.

With every opportunity I have to be with them, to
talk to them, or to write them, I can and will encourage
my loved ones to know the truth of Your constant,
loving presence.

I pray the prayer of faith—faith in You to bring my
loved ones through the day safe and healthy, faith in
them to be willing to turn to You throughout the day.

I pray for my loved ones and encourage them
to know the presence of God.

Day 191

—◆—

God has been so lavish in His gifts that you can lose
some priceless ones, the equivalent of whole kingdoms,
and still be indecently rich.—Wilfrid Sheed

PROSPERITY

My finances may not increase overnight, but my understanding of what constitutes my prosperity is certainly increasing.

For instance, I am learning every day that prosperity is much more than having enough money to pay bills or to buy things. I know that true prosperity is something I cannot earn or buy. It is something I have always had: the unlimited provision of God's grace.

I live my prosperity as a spiritual unity with God. Then I never limit or misuse my prosperity. My view of the world is from an understanding of my oneness with God and with all that God has created.

God is the source of all blessings. Family, friends, a beautiful planet on which to live—all are part of my unlimited prosperity.

> God, You are the source of all blessings
> and every enrichment in life.

Day 192

$\longrightarrow \blacklozenge \longrightarrow$

Be strong and of good courage.
—1 Chronicles 22:13

NOTHING TO FEAR In a message of assurance, God tells me: "You are never alone, beloved child, for I am always with you. I am with you through the darkest of nights, and I am with you as you celebrate your greatest triumphs.

"Whenever you need Me, I am here for you. If you are lonely or afraid, turn to Me. Feel My love as I encircle you in the warmth of My presence.

"Whenever you call, I will answer. You are a precious creation of Mine, and I will carry you over the rugged places on your path of life. I will never leave you, for it is My great desire to see you succeed.

"Beloved, you have nothing to fear. No matter what may be going on around you, know that you have Me to lean on. My spirit is within you; you are forever a part of Me. Together, we are one."

Whenever I call, God answers—with the assurance that I am loved.

Day 193

— ◆ —

The power that makes grass grow, fruit ripen,
and guides the bird in flight is in all of us.
—Anzia Yezierska

**I Am
Ready**

How amazing it is that with all the thoughts I think, one thought surfaces and launches me in a new direction in life! How astounding it is that a thought keeps occurring until I act on it—with such wonderful results that I wonder why I hesitated!

Yet, when I filter my thoughts through a spiritual awareness, I receive life-enhancing ideas and carry through with them. Spirit within lets me know I am ready for a challenge or a change. Such a holy confirmation gives me confidence.

I listen and hear a parable of Jesus echoing down through the ages to me: "Then the King will say . . . 'Come . . . inherit the kingdom prepared for you from the foundation of the world.'" (Matthew 25:34) My answer is "Yes," because I am ready for that kingdom now.

**Spirit lets me know I am ready for
the kingdom of God.**

DAILY WORD FOR FAMILIES

Day 194

—◆—

The natural world is dynamic. From the expanding universe to the hair on a baby's head, nothing is the same from now to the next moment.—Helen Hooven Santmyer

HEALING IS POSSIBLE

A healing can come in a variety of ways, such as the restoration of a relationship, the overcoming of fear, or the renewal of the body. All these healings are possible because the presence of God is within all of us.

So I claim healing now: I am healed of all emotional wounds that I have experienced, even as a child. My mind is free of negative thoughts that might have held me back from accepting the glorious possibilities each new day brings.

My relationships with others are peaceful and joy-filled, because the healing love of God is present within each of us. This same healing love causes me to think before I speak from any place other than love.

I am healed—mind and body. God created me to be whole and well and has infused the very cells of my body with life and renewal.

God is the answer to every need for healing.

DAILY WORD FOR FAMILIES

Day 195

—◆—

Dreams are . . . illustrations from the book
your soul is writing about you.
—Marsha Norman

THANK YOU, GOD! What inspires me the most? Other people and their stories of overcoming challenges motivate me. I consider that if they are able to have such strength, I can too.

Sometimes I even inspire myself—especially when I am able to do something that I had no idea I was capable of doing. I'm moved by sacred writings and poetry, by music and art, by sunrises and sunsets.

There are so many people, so many things that inspire me. I am excited about life! And out of that inspiration there is a growing feeling of thanksgiving. So I give thanks to God for each person, each word, each scene of nature that rouses me out of a feeling of complacency to the elation of thanksgiving. "Thank You, God, for inspiring me through all that You have created!"

Thank You, God, for inspiring me.

DAILY WORD FOR FAMILIES

For the Children

Hello God,

Something happened today that helped me know more about You. I was riding home in my school bus with the window down so I could feel the wind on my face. I held my hand up and felt the wind wrap itself around my fingers, but I couldn't hold on to it.

Then I thought about You, God, and how You are like the wind: I can feel You, but I cannot see You. Sometimes I feel You wrap Yourself around me, God, and then I am not afraid or confused. It's like I reach out to You with my thoughts, and You answer me, telling me that You are with me.

I didn't tell any of the other kids on the bus what I was feeling and thinking as we rode home. I felt like I had a secret I wanted to tell the whole world, and maybe some day I will. Until then, God, I'll just tell You. And God, thank You for listening to me. I know You are here with me now and always.

Day 197

—◆—

Feeling grateful or appreciative of someone or something in your life actually attracts more of the things that you appreciate and value into your life.—Christiane Northrup

GOD, I BELIEVE IN YOU

Wouldn't it be wonderful if I could pack all my problems into a bag and then throw them away, never to see them again?

Well, I can. When my faith is in God—not in outer appearances—I can overcome any problem that may come my way and eliminate it from my life.

I can when I do not question that I can. So I put aside any doubt by remembering that God loves me and that I do not doubt my Creator.

Yes, I believe in God with all my heart. I know that, literally, nothing is impossible for God. With faith in God within me, I discover that all I desire to accomplish is possible.

God, I believe in You and place my trust in You.

DAILY WORD FOR FAMILIES

Day 198

—◆—

All my life through, the new sights
of Nature made me rejoice like a child.
—Marie Curie

**VACATION
BLESSING**
A vacation can be an adventure of fun and activity. Or it can be a time to get away, leave behind everyday matters, and relax as I allow the spirit of God to renew me. This time of rest helps me prepare for the new experiences ahead.

Yet what do I do for rest and renewal when I cannot go away on a trip or take time away from my routine? Wherever I am, I take a moment to stop what I am doing and give any concern or frustration over to God. In those few moments with God, I feel at peace.

I know that any time can be a time of relaxation. I don't need a vacation or a trip to be refreshed. By simply becoming still and taking a journey of awareness to God, I am refreshed.

I am renewed in mind, body, and spirit.

DAILY WORD FOR FAMILIES

Day 199

*The most called-upon prerequisite
of a friend is an accessible ear.*
—*Maya Angelou*

**BEST
FRIEND**

Having someone to confide in is not only a relief, but also a help. A friend is an invaluable asset in life, but one that may not always be instantly available to me.

However, there is one who is always available and ready to listen to my ideas and to encourage me. This is my best friend, who guides me with a wisdom that far surpasses any I could find anywhere else. This friend, my best friend, is God.

God knows my concerns even before I can put words to my needs. Any actions I take can never truly be called my own, not when I am willing to let God be a part of all that I do.

God is the core of my being—the source of all that blesses me. I give thanks that God is my dearest friend.

**With God as my best friend and guide, I can
and do release all concern.**

Day 200

---◆---

Those who bring sunshine to the lives
of others cannot keep it from themselves.
—James Matthew Barrie

LIFE OF PRAYER

At some point and time, most people are placed in the role of a caregiver. Some are just starting a family, others are sending a child off to college, and still others are caring for a family member who is in need of assistance.

In thinking of my own role as a caregiver, I focus on God so that I won't become discouraged by problems or concerns. Then I am filled with the strength, love, and compassion I need to live my life and care about and for others.

I do not ask God for specific solutions; rather, I listen to the divine message that I know will come. God guides me to act responsibly and to share my joy of living with my loved ones.

My desire is to live my life as a sacred expression of prayer by sharing love with my family and friends. As I care about and for others, I live a life of prayer.

I live my life as a sacred expression
of prayer by sharing love.

Day 201

---◆---

Tolerance and celebration of individual differences
is the fire that fuels lasting love.
—Tom Hannah

**DIVERSITY** If all people were exactly alike—all looking alike, eating the same foods, living in the same manner—the lack of variety might make the world seem rather lackluster.

Thank God for diversity! I give thanks that there is diversity in my world and that my life is blessed with multitudes of interesting individuals.

I honor diversity. I give thanks to God for the blessing of my own individuality and the individuality of others. And in my everyday life, I revere and nourish the diversity of all people by being open and receptive to their uniqueness and traditions, their thoughts and insight.

Each day I let my words and actions be a reflection of the peace, patience, and love of God within me. My life is filled with the blessings of many unique individuals.

I appreciate and honor diversity!

Day 202

—◆—

*There's nothing that can help you understand your beliefs
more than trying to explain them to an inquisitive child.*
—Frank A. Clark

**DIVINE
POTENTIAL**

Each day, new life is entering the
world—precious beings who are
created by and enfolded in God's love,
who are nurtured by divine promise.
And while I will not have an opportunity to know each
one, I have a reverence for life that encourages me to
help build a better world for all children, for all people.

As I listen to divine wisdom, I am shown the ways
that I can be a blessing to people and to the world. I,
too, have divine promise within me to fulfill. I have
capabilities and potential that far exceed my own
expectations of myself. I have potential that I am ready
to discover and fulfill. The blessing that results is
something I share with others.

**By discovering and expressing my own potential,
I bless myself and others.**

Day 203

—◆—

The sun, with all those planets revolving around it and dependent on it, can still ripen a bunch of grapes as if it had nothing else in the universe to do.—Galileo

ORDER

God, I now realize so clearly that You love me unconditionally. Your love enfolds me and is constantly creating an environment of order for me to live in and from.

At times I may have felt as if I were being pulled into a sea of chaos around me. Then, I turned to You and discovered that I was supported by an atmosphere of divine order, which kept me buoyant and afloat.

Right now, here with You, I rest. I understand that there is always an answer to every dilemma, a way around any obstacle, and a source of order in every moment.

God, You are my peace in any turmoil. Because I know this, I listen for the sweet assurance that You are always giving me.

I am living in an orderly world that God created.

Day 204

—♦—

Every man's life is a fairy tale
written by God's finger.
—*Hans Christian Andersen*

FULLNESS OF LIFE
There have been times when I have felt as if something were missing in my favorite recipe, but I couldn't quite determine what it was. Maybe after reaching a long-awaited goal, I felt disappointed but didn't know why.

My likes and dislikes, my preferences and goals can change. However, when I have an urgent feeling that something in life itself is missing, what do I do?

Well, instead of looking to other people or to my own accomplishments, I turn to God, the very source of life. With an awareness of God, I find greater meaning in life and greater fulfillment in carrying out my part in the overall plan for all creation.

I appreciate the magnificence of all life and infuse my life with expectation. There can be nothing missing because, with God, I experience the fullness of life.

God, by knowing You, I experience the fullness of life.

Day 205

—◆—

*You will come to understand that because you are
the offspring of God, with freedom of choice, and with
command of the power, faculties, and qualities of being,
you can determine just what will come into your life.*
—*Myrtle Fillmore*

**HONOR
FREEDOM**

Knowing as much as possible about a situation can free me to make a decision based on accurate information. When I consider events from a larger perspective, I tend not to make snap judgments that I may later regret.

However, what can I do when I have few or no facts to rely on, when I may never know the full story about some person or situation? I am still free—free to choose what words to say or actions to take. And, most important, I am free to rely on God for the answers I seek.

God is with me to guide me through every circumstance. I rely on God to show me the way. Through divine freedom, I am free myself and I honor freedom for all people everywhere.

I am free and I honor the freedom of all people.

Day 206

Then your light shall break forth like the dawn,
and your healing shall spring up quickly.
—Isaiah 58:8

HEALING STREAM

The life of God shines within me every hour of the day and night. The radiant energy of divine life is eternal, and its healing glow bathes every cell of my body right now, giving me new energy and strength.

At all times, God's healing life is flowing through me in a soothing stream. I visualize it washing over me, cleansing my body of all impurities and transforming me—mind and body. I am whole. I feel strong and vitally alive!

Yes, God is always with me as life and strength in every cell of my being. I have the energy I need to complete whatever presents itself today, and I even have energy to spare. Every day, I am becoming healthier and more energetic as the life of God within continues to nourish and sustain me.

The life of God is healing me now.

Day 207

—◆—

*When beauty finally suffuses our soul, nothing else
will take precedence, because we will have discovered
the essence of God.—Charles Lelly*

**BEAUTY
OF SPIRIT**
God's spirit lives within me, and it is the spirit of God that fills me with peace and soothes away the stress of the day. I know that I am loved, that I am an important part of God's world.

Just as the sunflower turns to the warming rays of the early morning sun, I, too, turn to the light—the all-powerful presence of God within me. In God's presence, my awareness of my own spiritual identity unfolds so that the inner beauty of Spirit shines forth from me.

Such beauty of Spirit reveals itself as love and understanding, which are essential to me as I live, work with, and help others. I appreciate living in a world in which each person adds to the beauty of the whole.

**The beauty of Spirit shines forth from me
as love and understanding.**

Day 208

Spirituality leaps where science cannot yet follow, because science must always test and measure, and much of reality and human experience is immeasurable.—Starhawk

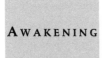

AWAKENING

Deep within my soul there is a stirring—an awakening to the sacredness that has always been there. This awakening is the knowledge that I am a divine creation.

I dedicate my thoughts and prayers to learning more of the spiritual attributes with which I have been blessed. In my prayers, I give thanks for the answers I am receiving to the questions that are on my mind.

Divine life in all its glory is being brought forth in expression in my life. My senses are totally attuned to the blessings around me. Every sight, smell, sound, texture, and taste in life awakens me to the glory of God. With this awakening, I feel my oneness with God's glory. I am one with absolute wisdom and eternal love.

My soul is awakened to the glory of Spirit.

Day 209

---◆---

*When you find peace within yourself, you become
the kind of person who can live at peace with others.*
—Peace Pilgrim

**W O R L D
V I S I O N**

How can I bless the world? I hold a vision for the world—a vision of peace and love. I see all people trusting and accepting one another. United in a sense of purpose, people are working together to accomplish great things for the benefit of all.

There is a worldwide dedication to healing planet Earth so that all nature and all natural wonders not only survive but flourish. This is a world in which all people live together in harmony.

I know this vision of the world can become a reality. I help with that reality by helping to create an environment of peace in my home and immediate surroundings. Such a vision of peace is shared by others so that, person by person, family by family, peace circles the globe. World peace can be a reality, and I do what I can to help it along the way.

**My commitment is to helping create a world
of peace and love.**

Day 210

Circle of Love

What could bring more delight to our hearts than sharing joy with our families and friends? What relieves us more of our burdens than when someone helps us carry them for a while?

There is no question about it. We are in this life together. Ours is a commitment of family— a commitment that reaches out to everyone who is willing to be loved and to love in return. Sometimes we walk the journey of life together throughout a lifetime. Sometimes we are together to help each other over the rough spots and up to the high places.

What an honor it is to share life. As we look around at each other and think of those who, although separated from us, are always fresh in our thoughts, we know we are fulfilling a divine plan. God has brought us together to help each other and to be blessed in giving and receiving love.

We are one, after all, you and I. Together we suffer, together exist, and forever will recreate each other.
—Pierre Teilhard de Chardin

THE GIFT OF LIFE, THE GIFT OF UNCONDITIONAL LOVE

BY MAURICE WILLIAMS

I met my younger brother Eric at the airport on a hot July day in 1987. I love my brother, but this time the quality of my life, my life itself, depended on him—if he could pass the test.

My life had started to change drastically in April 1981. Back then I was attending evening classes at both a ministerial school and a local community college and working 10 to 12 hours a day as a carpenter; I was understandably tired. But when an overwhelming lack of energy persisted, I decided to have a thorough physical examination. Afterward, I was stunned by what my doctor told me: "Maurice, you have irreversible kidney failure."

I began four hours of dialysis three times a week while continuing ministerial and community college classes. After receiving a college degree, I needed to finish my ministerial training at Unity Village, Missouri, but I told one of my teachers, "I'm going to stay here in Detroit until I'm healed."

She responded, "The same God who will heal you in Detroit will heal you at Unity Village."

Six months later at Unity, I received a telephone call

at 2:30 A.M. A doctor asked if I wanted a new kidney.

The surgery went well, and in June I graduated from ministerial school and was ordained. That October, I was accepted as the minister of a Unity church in Nassau, Bahamas.

Then, for some reason, my body began to reject the new kidney. Sadly, I left the church in Nassau and returned to Kansas City for more dialysis.

My mother called and encouraged me to ask my brother Eric to be a donor.

"Mom," I replied, "Eric knows I need a kidney. If he wants to give me one, he'll tell me. And, Mom, how healthy can his kidneys be? You know that Eric is a good-time man, and he's overweight, too! I don't think he could possibly pass the physical to be a donor."

But my mother persisted, so I finally gave in and called Eric, who lived in Detroit. I asked him if he would be my donor. Without even a second thought he said: "I'll be glad to give you a kidney."

My heart sank as I watched Eric sort of roll off the plane that day in 1987. He was overweight, bulging out of his three-piece suit so much that he had popped two buttons. My faith was at a low ebb. He looked at me and said, "I came here to give you a kidney, and I'm not leaving until I do."

After Eric had his physical, the doctor said, "He's a perfect match; the best donor you could ever hope for."

I blurted out, "Are you sure you're talking about my brother, Eric Williams?"

"He's great," said the doctor. "We can't give any donor a score of 100 percent, but we gave Eric a 98!"

That taught me a lesson: When God is ready to bring your good to you, God will do it in spite of your own faith or lack of it. What I have learned and am still learning from Eric is something that I could never learn in any school: unconditional love.

Eric was wheeled into the operating room just ahead of me. With my mother, father, and some friends standing nearby, he said something that touched my heart: "Maurice, I'm giving you this kidney because I love you." Then he said something that touched my soul: "And Maurice, God is giving you this kidney because God loves you."

All these years since then, my health has been good. It is a gift. My perception of Eric for a time was limiting, but Eric gave me a part of himself and the gift of unconditional love. That is something we all have to live in order to give. The gift of unconditional love blesses us first before it reaches out to bless others.

Eric helped me know this truth: With God, all things are possible. I have embraced this truth and share it in my ministry with anyone who is willing to listen. I encourage everyone to never, never criticize any child of God, for each one is a potential channel for good, a giver of unconditional love.

Day 211

The ones that give,
get back in kind.
—Pam Durban

**GIVE
AND
RECEIVE**
I feel such joy when I see the look of wonder and excitement on the face of a child who is unwrapping a gift I have given. Drawn into this magical moment, I sense the excitement that is building. As if one in mind and heart with the child, I share the joy of giving and receiving.

Yet I have so much more to give than material gifts. When I give from the heart—love and compassion—I give something of greater value than any package can hold. I give a part of myself, sharing joyfully from my spiritual nature.

In giving a gift of spirit, I receive a great blessing in return. Joy and peace bless me in "good measure, pressed down, shaken together, running over." (Luke 6:38)

**I both give and receive from the love
of God within me.**

Day 212

—◆—

May mercy, peace, and love
be yours in abundance.
—Jude 1:2

ABUNDANCE OF LOVE
One of my greatest joys is being with family and friends, sharing memories of times past and experiences of the present.

In our times of sharing, the love that God has placed within our hearts moves out through smiles and laughter, compassionate thoughts and encouraging words. This is the atmosphere of love I want in my home at all times so that it will be a haven of peace.

And it can be. When I let my thoughts be of God, there is an abundance of love in my home. The welcome mat is out so that everyone who enters my home is greeted by the very presence of divine love in expression.

Abundant love creates an atmosphere of acceptance and peace in my home.

Day 213

———◆———

A true companion is always available
no matter what the circumstances.
—Arvella Schuller

TRAVELING COMPANION   God, wherever I am, wherever I go—on the earth, in the air, or on the waters—You are with me. I feel such peace in Your holy presence that I am calm and my decisions are clear.

Especially while traveling, I appreciate being free of confusion and anxiety. I enjoy the scenery and the people who are traveling with me. I am able to make adjustments for unexpected circumstances and last-minute changes.

I remember, God, to take along my sense of humor on both short trips and long journeys. I can never really be a stranger or alone, for You are my guide and divine companion. Your presence is in every new city or country so that I am always on holy ground.

God is my constant companion.

Day 214

—◆—

It is your privilege to be as free
as the birds, the trees, the flowers.
—Charles Fillmore

CELEBRATION OF SPIRIT The greatest freedom I can ever experience is the freedom coming from the knowledge that the spirit of God is an innate part of me.

When God whispers gently, quietly to me, "You are free," I respond with a jubilation that moves me beyond any thought of limitation. I am free!

No boundaries can limit me and no person can keep me from expressing the divine qualities with which I have been blessed. I am free!

I understand that freedom of Spirit is a reality for everyone—not just me. God speaks to every person. I pray that people throughout the world listen to God's message of freedom and celebrate the freedom that comes from realizing the presence of God. We are all free!

I celebrate freedom of Spirit!

Day 215

—◆—

Dreams are renewable. No matter what our age
or condition, there are still untapped possibilities within us
and new beauty waiting to be born.—Dale Turner

**SOUL
SATISFACTION**

How do I satisfy a feeling of wanting something when I don't know what that something is? At times I may have mistaken that longing for a material need or a career achievement and then been disappointed when I achieved or received what I thought I wanted or needed.

Now I know I can leave mistakes and disappointments behind when I recognize that my greatest longing is from my soul. What brings my soul the greatest satisfaction is knowing the presence of God.

So I take time every day to stop what I am doing and become quiet. In that quiet, I know the presence of God with my total being. In the quiet, aware of God, the longing of my soul is satisfied. What a blessing the fulfillment of my soul is!

God, You alone satisfy the longing of my soul.

Day 216

—◆—

*I go into the wilderness
and rediscover the home within.*
—*China Galland*

PEACEFUL REDISCOVERY

After I have returned from a journey, I find great comfort in rediscovering the sights of neighborhood and home. Whether I am at home or away, I can feel the same reassurance of being home when I turn within to the peace of God.

God's presence is within me and goes before me. From the rising of the sun each morning to the twinkling of the stars at night, the signs and wonders of God are all around me. These familiar signs comfort me.

I can speak to God at any time about concerns I may have, or I can say a heartfelt "thank You" for the blessings in my life. God is my strength and comfort in every situation and in whatever I am doing, and I can always go home.

The signs and wonders of God comfort me.

DAILY WORD FOR FAMILIES

Day 217

—◆—

Our consciousness rarely registers the beginning
of a growth within us any more than without us: there
have been many circulations of the sap before we detect
the smallest sign of the bud.—Mary Ann Evans

STARTING OVER

Now or at some time in the future, I may feel as if I am starting over. I might be making a career change, ending or beginning a relationship, or even moving from one home to another. But whatever the circumstances, I will be starting over with a familiar friend—God.

I may be uncertain about what the future holds for me, but I can have true peace of mind when I rely on God for support and know that the right outcome is already in motion.

The thought of starting over does not intimidate me, for I have the highest counsel I could ever hope to have—the loving presence of God.

With God guiding me, starting over is simply starting fresh. Exhilaration fills me, and I greet each day with eager anticipation.

At every turning point, God is with me.

Day 218

— ◆ —

Act as if what you do makes a difference.
It does.
—William James

AMAZING ME

I may feel embarrassed thinking of myself as an amazing person. However, I feel inspired when I realize that the reason I am amazing is not because of anything I have done; it is because of what God has done in creating me.

In fact, the world is full of amazing people. We may look different and sound different, but we have something amazing in common: the spirit of God that is the very life we are living.

Knowing this, I can never take myself or another person for granted. I can never limit what I or another person can achieve when I understand that the life and wisdom of God are being lived out in wonderful and amazing ways through us.

I am one of God's creations of wonder
and amazement.

Day 219

—◆—

They say, "You can't give a smile away; it always comes back." The same is true of a kind word or a conversation starter. What goes around, comes around.—Susan RoAne

GOLDEN RULE
Jesus gave unqualified love and felt endless compassion for everyone. I can imagine Him looking out at the crowds and understanding individual needs as He tenderly searched each face.

He gave people hope and insight into their inner spiritual power and glory. He taught His disciples simple but powerful principles that all could understand and apply in their lives—down through the ages.

One of those principles is the Golden Rule, and oh, how it blesses me each time I use it in my life! When I give the consideration and kindness I want to receive, I not only feel good about what I am doing, but I feel refreshed as well—both emotionally and physically.

I give the love and kindness to others that I want to receive from them.

Day 220

—◆—

God is the same yesterday,
today, and forever.
—Cora Dedrick Fillmore

DIVINE ASSURANCE God assures me: "Beloved child, know that I am the source of all you need to feel at peace within and about yourself.

"I love you, and I am always with you. At any time and in any circumstance, you have only to be consciously aware of Me in order to find Me. I am ready to give you constant assurance.

"Know the truth: You will never need to face anything on your own, for I am right there with you. As you trust in Me completely, you will satisfy the desire of your soul, for you will know I am a part of you and you are a part of Me.

"Never lose hope, beloved; rest in the assurance of My love and care. I will always be with you, encouraging you and guiding you in fulfilling your dreams."

God is with me always, giving me the assurance
of divine love and care.

Day 221

—◆—

Love is not a doctrine. Peace is not an international agreement. Love and peace are beings who live as possibilities in us.—Mary Caroline Richards

AMBASSADOR OF LOVE AND PEACE The peace I feel within my heart and soul stirs up such joy that I just naturally want to share it with everyone around me.

I let the peace of God speak through me so that my words are always kind. It is natural that when I speak to others with love, they respond in kind.

The peace of God moves through me when I interact with other people or with nature. God is guiding me, so I know that my actions are divinely inspired.

I am an ambassador of God's love to others because I am aware of the peace I feel in my own heart. I understand that inner peace can only come from the presence of God.

The peace of God within me fills me with serenity.

Day 222

—◆—

Motivation is like food for the brain. You cannot get enough in one sitting. It needs continual and regular top-ups.—Peter Davies

NOURISH THE SOUL I nourish my body daily with food, and I nourish my mind with the facts and information I am constantly learning. Yet how often do I nourish my soul?

Nourishing my soul is so simple, so easy, that I may tend to overlook how I can do it. What my soul needs is for me to be aware of God. I attain this awareness as I think of God—the spirit of God within me and all around me. As I pray, I feel an undeniable oneness with my Creator.

"God, You are my life, my wisdom, my peace. What strength I realize when I am aware of You! You are the air I breathe, the life I give expression to, the understanding I need to live life fully. Thank You, God, for nourishing me—spirit, body, and soul."

Thank You, God, for nourishing my soul.

Day 223

—◆—

When we are aware of our oneness with God,
nothing is impossible to us, no matter what outer
appearances may indicate.—Donald Curtis

UNITY OF SPIRIT

At this moment around the world, some people are waking up, others are still asleep, and still others are already busy at work or school. Some of us will give thanks for a cloudless sky and sunshine; others will give thanks for gentle rain that nourishes the soil. Yet we are all under the same sky, sharing the same air. And we also share a sacred unity of spirit.

We do not all think alike, and most of us do not even look alike. We are all unique and distinctive. Whether we pray in the same fashion by speaking the same words or following the same motions, our intentions are the same—to remain in tune with the wisdom and truth of God.

In a unity of spirit, we are family—one with each other and one with God.

This is a golden day—a day to celebrate
our unity of spirit.

Day 224

---◆---

*The events in our lives happen in a sequence in time,
but in their significance to ourselves they find
their own order . . . the continuous thread of revelation.*
—*Eudora Welty*

**IMMERSED
IN GOD**

The second I realize I am letting myself be drawn into any disorder around me, I know to become quiet and focus inward. Then I give my full attention to God.

Out of my quiet time, a realization of calm rises within me. The people, the noise, and the confusion that seemed right in my face have retreated. I feel such relief that I breathe easier. I relax, and the tension in my arms and shoulders melts.

To be fully conscious of God is to be immersed in the order God is continually providing for me. My responsibility is to be aware of the order that is always there and to flow with it. What a wonderful surrender this is. I am giving up worry and stress and allowing myself to be immersed in God's order and peace.

**In a time of quiet, I am immersed
in the order and peace of God.**

Day 225

—◆—

At any time, an entirely new possibility is liable to come along and spin you off in an entirely new direction. The trick, I've learned, is to be awake to the moment.
—Doug Hall

DIVINE POSSIBILITIES

Throughout childhood, I looked forward to a time when I would graduate from school and begin to experience life rather than merely learn about it. However, I have since discovered that learning is a natural part of experiencing life—every day of my life, no matter how old I am.

And just as I am constantly discovering something new about my life and my world, I am continually being guided to new doors of opportunity. As each new door appears, I trust that God is presenting me with a new chapter of learning.

With God as my teacher, I am a student of divine possibilities and never-ending adventures.

God opens doors of opportunity to me, and my faith leads me through them.

Day 226

For the Children

Hello God,

I wasn't feeling very good yesterday—until I tried an experiment. This is what I did: Every time I started thinking about how bad I felt, I switched to thinking about You. At first I didn't notice any difference, but guess what? The more I thought about You, the less I thought about what was bothering me. Then it wasn't bothering me at all!

Were You thinking about me while I was thinking about You, God? Is that why I started feeling so much better? I've decided I'm going to do this whenever I have a problem. If someone is not nice to me at school, I'm going to think about You and how nice You are. If I'm feeling sad or just not in a good mood, I'm going to think about You so I'll have happy thoughts!

Is this what Mom and Dad mean by "let go and let God"? That's what I'm going to do from now on—and boy, do I feel better already!

Day 227

—◆—

We cannot always control our thoughts, but we can control our words. Repetition impresses the subconscious, and we are then master of the situation.—Florence Scovel Shinn

HEALING WORDS

There is great power in words. At times it's as if the very cells of my body are listening to what I have to say. I feel the words throughout my body as I say them and feel their effect linger in my body after I have spoken them.

So I make a conscious effort to speak words that are messages of healing to my heart and lungs, to my joints and muscles, to my nerves and digestive system. I can literally feel a response as I encourage my heart to beat in perfect rhythm and my lungs to take in oxygen and send it to all areas of my body.

My message for myself is composed of words of health and healing and has as its source the very Spirit of life within me. I nourish my body with words of life and give thanks for the amazing results.

I bless my body with words of life and healing.

Day 228

Light is the reality of God
within all creation.
—Eric Butterworth

LIVING IN GOD'S LIGHT God speaks to me in the silence of prayer, and I listen. I listen with an open mind and heart as God gives me the guidance I need to live a joy-filled life. Then I proclaim the truth about me: I am living in God's radiant light of understanding. I have a new vision—a vision of what my life can and will be through the blessings of God's grace.

I am living in God's radiant light of understanding. Bathed in the warm glow of God's love, I have confidence. God is with me in every moment, giving me the courage to accomplish whatever is mine to accomplish.

I am living in God's radiant light of understanding. Peace radiates from me and shines on the path of life before me. Each step I take leads me forward, and always the glow of God's love is there to greet me.

I am living in God's radiant light of understanding.

Day 229

—◆—

The dedicated life is worth living.
You must give with your whole heart.
—Annie Dillard

ZEST FOR LIVING

When I hear the joyful laughter of a child or the cheerful song of a bird, I am inspired by the zest for life being expressed.

When I see the beauty of an unfolding rose or the compassion of a caregiver who is reaching out to someone needing to be consoled, I feel a surge of appreciation for life.

These are reminders, but the source of my enthusiasm is within me. My inner spiritual nature is always ready to spring forth—to inspire me, strengthen me, and direct me in living life fully and completely.

My life is an adventure in living when I open my soul and let the boundless enthusiasm of my spiritual nature be expressed as energy and love. I allow the beauty and power of Spirit to come forward in all that I do in life.

I am enthusiastic about life!

Day 230

— ◆ —

Use what talent you possess: the woods would be
very silent if no birds sang except those that sang best.
—*Henry Van Dyck*

NEEDED AND IMPORTANT God speaks to me in the quiet of my soul: "You are My creation, and I love you. There is nothing you could ever do that would make Me love you less, for I am pure love in expression. You can never be separated from Me or from My love and care.

"So whenever a challenge seems too big for you to handle, remember who you are—My child. Remember that you are needed and important and that without you, the world would not be complete.

"The beauty of your soul shines brightly as a beacon of My love to the people around you. Let your light shine as a reminder to everyone of their own importance in the order and harmony of the world. Remember who you are and all that you can do to bless the world with your presence."

I am a needed and important part of God's world.

Day 231

—◆—

Think of the magic of that foot comparatively small,
upon which your whole weight rests. It's a miracle,
and the dance . . . is a celebration of that miracle.
—Martha Graham

GOD'S MIRACLE The miracles of abundance and healing proclaim the truth of God's presence. I have only to look around me to see the glory of God's presence in my life.

For instance, when I look in the mirror, what do I see? I see me—one of God's miracles! As a beloved child of God, I am a miracle of light and life and love.

Then I look around me. The miracle of God shines brightly in every face I encounter, in every bit of nature with which I come into contact.

Miracles are happening because God is the power
and presence in all life!

Day 232

—◆—

Life is a great big canvas, and you
should throw all the paint you can on it.
—Danny Kaye

C H A N G E

No matter how well other people know me, they may not know what is best for me. I may listen to their suggestions but decide not to follow through on them.

However, there is one who knows me far better than any other. So I listen to God's guidance and have faith that golden opportunities are being revealed to me.

When I make a change in my life, it is because I have been encouraged by an inner prompting to follow a new plan. Divine guidance may come as a gradual knowing or as a definite nudge in the right direction at an important turning point in my life.

I recognize divine guidance because I attune myself to God in prayer. Then I feel a confirmation in my soul that what I am receiving is the wisdom of God.

God knows and shows me what is best for me.

Day 233

—◆—

There are no problems—
only opportunities to be creative.
—Dorye Roettger

DIVINE SOLUTIONS I have faith in God! Just saying these words infuses me with confidence, because I hear my own words of faith echoing back to me.

I have faith in God within me. When I consider the intricate workings of my body, I am astounded. Just watching the beautiful synchronization with which my fingers and thumbs work together as I dig in the soil or turn the pages of a book is incredible.

Seemingly insurmountable obstacles shrink as I allow my faith in God to increase. Faith helps me to stay calm because it allows me to envision divinely inspired solutions as they take form and become a reality. With faith in God, I expect and accept the blessings of God—every day.

With faith in God, I envision divine solutions
that become a reality.

Day 234

All people are one in Spirit.
—Russel W. Lake

GENTLE SPIRIT

God's spirit is within me, and it is this gentle spirit of love and goodwill that ignites my desire to be loving and kind to others.

How could I be anything but gentle and kind when I am expressing God's love within me out into the world? God's spirit is at the core of every person. It is the very essence of our being—the inner nature that encourages us and enables us to treat one another with love and understanding.

It is God's gentle spirit within me that prepares me to be a messenger of peace—a messenger of kindness to myself and others. As I let God work in and through me, the tenderness and care of Spirit become a part of who I am and what I see in the world around me.

I am one with God's gentle, loving spirit.

Day 235

—◆—

If you are still being hurt by an event that happened to you at twelve, it is the thought that is hurting you now.
—James Hillman

WILLING TO FORGIVE

Which brings greater healing to a troubled soul: giving or receiving forgiveness?

I may or may not receive the words of forgiveness I long to hear from someone, but I can always give forgiveness—to myself and others. The very act of forgiving cleanses away irritating thoughts and begins a soothing, healing activity.

I give a boost to the health of my mind and body as I remain willing to give and receive forgiveness. The days seem brighter, and my relationships are enhanced by the love and harmony conveyed in forgiveness.

As I step forward to forgive, I may find that others are willing to meet me halfway. We are drawn together in mutual caring. How wonderful it is that such cooperation enhances my already stable relationships and restores the ones which need to be healed!

I am willing to forgive and to be forgiven.

DAILY WORD FOR FAMILIES

Day 236

—◆—

I believe that in our constant search for security,
we can never gain any peace of mind until we secure
our own soul.—Margaret Chase Smith

POWER TO BLESS
If my plan for peace of mind is simply letting go of worry, I may feel that I am giving up—on a goal, on myself, or on another person.
However, an assurance of peace washes over me when I let go and then let God be God in my life and in the lives of my loved ones.

Just how do I do this? I let go of worry and then imagine myself giving the challenge or situation to God for the right solution. I take nothing back that I have given to God.

Letting go and letting God, I am doing something that has the power to help me and to help others. I will think more clearly and act with more compassion. I will have a more positive, uplifting attitude, and the people around me will welcome my encouragement and support.

As I let go and let God, I use the power to bless.

DAILY WORD FOR FAMILIES

Day 237

---◆---

The more we pray, the more we experience the grace of God, until we finally realize that we live by grace.
—*Hypatia Hasbrouck*

RECOGNITION

God, Your grace assures me that I am loved unconditionally. You trust me to act in responsible ways, and that trust is a part of Your grace in action.

Although at times I have prayed fervently for Your help, I now understand that You were helping me all the time. All I needed to do was recognize and accept Your guidance.

I also realize that even before I pray, You provide the answer. My prayers comfort me and awaken me totally to Your presence. Then I know unquestionably that I live in an atmosphere which is saturated with Your grace.

God, You understand me. You allow me to learn from my mistakes and to grow in Your wisdom. Thank You, God, for Your grace in every moment of life.

**By recognizing the grace of God,
I know unconditional love.**

Day 238

— ◆ —

*I very much believe success is a personal thing,
very much dependent on how much a person deals with
and approaches both opportunities and crises.*
—Millie J. Kronflu

**DIVINE
APPOINTMENT**

Today is a day of new discoveries—
a day in which opportunities will
abound for me.

I am not here by happenstance—
I am here in this time and this place by divine
appointment. Because God has blessed me with a
creative mind and a willing spirit, I am eager to explore
the possibilities that this day holds.

My friends and loved ones may wonder why my
attitude is lighter and my face is brighter. This is
because I have a hope that is born of my faith in God.

I live in the here and now, grateful for this day and
this moment. With a celebration of thanksgiving, I
open my mind and heart to experiencing the blessings
of God.

This is my divine appointment day.

Day 239

◆

*Power is freedom. Power allows us to accomplish what
is important to us, in the manner that we best see fit.
It separates the doers from the dreamers.*
—Patti F. Mancini

UPLIFTING POWER   I am free—and I declare my freedom from any negative habits, from any discomfort or concern over events of the past.

I have not only gone through some experiences, I have also grown through them. I have learned that the spirit of God within me enables me to overcome habits or thoughts which at one time may have seemed to be huge obstacles to my happiness.

Now I know that no habit has the power to control me or limit me. There is only one power—the power of God—and this power uplifts me so that I can take a firm stand on matters of importance.

I am free! I am free! I am free! Affirming my freedom strengthens my resolve to remain free. The power of God is within me. Knowing this truth about myself, I believe in my own freedom so much that I live a life of freedom.

God's power uplifts me, and I am free!

Day 240

Circle of Love

God is the source of all joy, the joy within us that responds to people and events. So let us feel the joy of love within our family and friendships. We are special blessings from God who make each other's lives more fulfilling and complete.

As members of our family, we bless each other, for we were created by God to be a blessing. When we give freely of the love that fills our hearts—the love that looks beyond appearances and past grudges to the spirit of God within everyone—we join with each other in a circle of love.

Our circle of love is expanding! How uplifting it is to know that by doing what we can in our own lives, we are affecting the lives of each other. We are joining together in a true communion of love and caring.

Make my joy complete: be of the same mind,
having the same love, being in full accord
and of one mind.
—Philippians 2:2

ONE FAMILY
BY JANIE WRIGHT

Mommy, why do I look so different from you and daddy?"

As the mother of a daughter of mixed heritage, I had known that such a question would eventually come up, but I wasn't prepared for it so soon. She was only four years old.

Looking at my daughter, I decided to bypass the simple explanation and tell her instead what I've always believed in my heart to be true: "You look different because God took the very best from me and the very best from your daddy and made a very special, very beautiful little girl named Natalie."

Natalie has always had amazing insight for a child, but I still wondered how she would react to my explanation. Her reply wasn't long in coming: "But you told me that God makes *everybody* special."

"That's true," I replied.

"I guess I'm not so different after all, huh?"

And so began her fascination with the myriad colors and textures and shapes and sizes that make up the human family. "Why are some people so tall?" "Why are some people so pale?" "Why can't some people walk like the rest of us do?"

I could see that her curiosity was her way of learning more about herself, of discovering where she fit into the overall picture. So I answered her questions as best I could and trusted that God would give her the understanding she needed.

As time passed by, it became fairly routine for perfect strangers to come up to Natalie and tell her how beautiful she is. Never once did anyone make fun of her heritage or treat her any differently than the other kids in the neighborhood.

I was extremely grateful but wondered if eventually the issue of race would come up. I prayed that if it did, it would not be until Natalie was old enough to understand the fears other people have.

But my wish was not to be. One day when Natalie was five, she was playing outside with several neighborhood children when one little girl suddenly stopped playing with Natalie. She refused to play with her unless Natalie explained why her skin looked different.

Her demand caught the attention of several other children, and they all formed a circle around Natalie to hear what she had to say.

I didn't know what to do. I wanted to grab my little girl up in my arms and protect her from what I thought was going to be a painful experience. But something held me back.

As the circle of children closed in around her, Natalie

held up her arm. In a very firm voice, she ordered her friends to hold up their arms, too. Taken by surprise, they complied.

Pale arms, tanned arms, freckled arms, arms with scratches and even one with a cast on it appeared within the circle.

"Now look at our arms," she said. "None of them look alike. God made us all different, and we are all beautiful to God. But God made a very special little girl, and her name is Natalie."

At that moment, I knew that race was never going to be an issue with Natalie, because to Natalie the issue doesn't exist. She understands that God created us all to be unique, special in our own way. And we all have a contribution to make to the worldwide family of God. As Natalie says, "I have the biggest family in the world—one big family under God."

Day 241

It should be encouraging to you to know that if you are now confronted by any kind of problem . . . there is a way to solve it, and you will find the way . . . as surely as you apply to it the principles of divine truth.—Grenville Kleiser

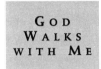

GOD WALKS WITH ME

Snuggling under a cover in the shelter of my home on a cold, rainy night is a great comfort to me. Yet— wherever I am, whatever I am doing—I have this same sense of well-being when I think of how God's presence is always surrounding me.

I can never be outside the presence of God. When I walk, God walks with me. During my waking hours, I release all concerns to God's care through prayer. I prepare myself for a restful night of sleep by gently affirming: *The presence of God surrounds me.* While I sleep, I am cared for by God.

Awake or asleep, at home or away, I know that God's constant, loving presence is always with me, and any concern is put to rest.

The presence of God surrounds me day and night.

Day 242

—◆—

Positive thoughts . . .
have positive results.
—Peter McWilliams

BLESSING OTHERS

I will play many roles in my life—parent, grandparent, caregiver—and I want what is best for my children and for all the children of the world. Children, more than anyone, embody hopes and dreams for the future and for peace on Earth.

As a caring individual, I know that it is a sacred responsibility to give love and support where it is needed. All children of God need hope—at whatever stage of life they may be experiencing.

From infants to senior citizens, all they may need in order to regain their momentum is the encouragement of a loving smile or a thoughtful word. Yes, even now, God-life in me is comforting and encouraging those around me.

God is working through me in
marvelous ways to bless others.

Day 243

—◆—

I went to the root of things,
and found nothing but Him alone.
—Mira Bai

PEACE OF MIND

What brings me the greatest peace of mind? Is it being with family and friends, completing a project, or receiving a good report about my health? All of the above are important; however, peace of mind is more than the absence of concern or worry. Knowing that God within me is my peace, my hope, my life is a thought which surges throughout my body, relaxing every nerve and muscle.

From the deepest recesses of my being, the peace of God rises to the surface of my awareness. As quickly as a dry sponge absorbs water, my body takes peace, glorious peace, into every cell.

Ah, this is how it feels to give inner peace total, unrestricted access to me. This feeling of absolute serenity is the peace of God within me, living out through me.

The peace of God is a serenity of the soul
that fills my mind and body.

Day 244

—◆—

Spirit is the real and eternal; matter
is the unreal and temporal.
—Mary Baker Eddy

BLESSED BY GOD

The enrichment of God's spirit permeates all I am, all I have, and all I do. I am so blessed by God. If the invisible activity of God were made visible, I would be dazzled by the energy, love, and care being expressed by the Creator on my behalf.

God has blessed me with life, and I live my life in thanksgiving to God. God has blessed me with wisdom, and I use this wisdom for the good of all humanity. God has blessed me with peace, and from that peace I live in harmony with others and my environment.

God never ceases to bless me. I live in an abundant world, sheltered, healed, and otherwise cared for by my loving Creator. Each day, I learn more and more of the ways that God blesses me.

I live in an abundant world, blessed by God
in every way.

Day 245

—◆—

Kind words can be short and easy to speak,
but their echoes are truly endless.
—Mother Teresa

COMMU-NICATION

God speaks through me as divine ideas concerning all that I may experience in life. And I keep in mind that God not only speaks through me, but through others as well. Therefore, whether I am at work or school or visiting with friends, I respect those I am with by paying attention to what they have to say.

As a good communicator, I allow words of love and understanding to flow from my lips. As a good listener, I focus all my attention and listen for gems of wisdom. I talk in gentle, understanding tones and do not interrupt when others are talking.

The more I follow God's guidance, the easier it becomes for me to keep the lines of communication with others open. In an atmosphere of love and understanding, my conversations with others flow smoothly.

God speaks through me in a language
of peace and goodwill.

Day 246

The light is with you.
—John 12:35

COMPLETE HEALING

The spirit of God is continuously moving through my body, healing and restoring every cell and fiber. At the same time, God is also healing my mind of any condition caused by negative thoughts, stress, or concern.

I am alert to the life of God in me! With the "clutter" of everyday concerns gone, creative, productive thoughts have a chance to grow and take root in my mind. With God showing me what I need to do, I use my energy to turn my expectations into reality.

I maintain a healthy state of mind by establishing as my priority a daily routine of quiet times of relaxation and intimate talks with God. I make a commitment to relax and let the healing life of God have full access to my mind. Leading a spiritually satisfying life, I am enriched both mentally and physically.

Alert to the life of God within me,
I am healed—mind and body.

Day 247

—◆—

*There will come a time when you believe everything
is finished. That will be the beginning.*
—Louis L'Amour

**FAITH
IS A
BRIDGE** Every ending is a prelude to a new
beginning. There is great truth in this
statement. Yet if I allow it to happen, I
can let the comfort of my familiar
routines keep me from stepping forward to experience
something even more fulfilling.

So I consider this: I am a work in progress, and the
Creator is constantly giving me the strength and
wisdom I need for each new beginning. I have faith
in God, and knowing that my Creator never gives up
on me, I never give up on myself or on my hopes and
my dreams.

My faith in God is a bridge that takes me from every
ending to a new beginning. I know without a doubt
that God is with me, guiding me successfully through
every challenge and through every change.

**Thank You, God, for being with me
in every new beginning.**

Day 248

—◆—

Appreciation of life itself, becoming suddenly aware of the miracle of being alive . . . can turn what we call ordinary life into a miracle. We come awake to such a realization when we recognize our connection to a spiritual dimension.—Dan Wakefield

GLORY OF GOD

Oh, what beauty of Spirit there is in the world! Everywhere I turn, I see the glory of God; the wonder of the Creator fills me with awe and inspiration.

And yet, of all the beauty and wonder, none fills me with the same sense of glory I feel when I consider the precious gift of life that has been given to me. My life has divine origins, and the spirit of God continues to act as my guide and my comfort, my support and my strength.

I am filled with the glory of Spirit! I hope that all who see me will also see the light of God radiating from me. Peace of mind lightens my step, and I stand taller. My presence speaks to others of their own inner strength— the glory of God that shines in all.

I am filled with the glory of God!

Day 249

—◆—

I have a need inside me, of a certain joy, you see?
An expression of joy. I feel it. I suppose that I am glad
to be alive. . . . And I hope everybody has that feeling
inside. I am grateful that I have a spirit inside me
which often sings.—Nina Holton

GRATITUDE

God, You give me the love and comfort I need to make it through any time of adjustment and change. As I pray, I hear You whisper that You are my strength. Thank You for reminding me that You are a never-ending source of healing, comfort, and peace. Nothing can bring me down, because You are constantly building me up in body, mind, and spirit.

When I consider all that You have done and continue to do for me, I can't help but be filled with gratitude and joy. Thank You, God, for welcoming me home to the comfort of Your presence every time I need to rest, to heal, or to give expression to my gratitude for You.

**I am grateful that God always welcomes me
with the love and comfort I seek.**

Day 250

—◆—

The love of our neighbor in all its fullness
simply means being able to say to him, "What are
you going through?"—Simone Weil

KINSHIP OF SPIRIT As I pray for the ones I love, I give thanks for them. They have given me so much reason for joy and have added meaning to my life.

So wherever they go and whatever they may do, I keep them in my thoughts and prayers. I share a kinship of spirit with them, and I am continually affirming that they are surrounded by the light and love of God.

Whenever my dear ones need me, I will support them with love and my highest hopes for their well-being. I will help them when I can and stand beside them always. I am praying for them and giving thanks as they continue to be the expressions of divine love that God created them to be.

In a kinship of spirit with family and friends,
I pray for them.

Day 251

---◆---

Freedom is knowing who
you really are.
—Linda Thomson

EMBRACING FREEDOM   I need never worry about being free of a habit or way of life that may not be the best for me, because I know that freedom is mine. I claim my freedom now, for in spirit, I am already free—free to do and be whatever I desire.

The power of God is within me, for the spirit of God is within all people. One with God, I am one with the spiritual freedom that is a part of my divine nature. I joyfully embrace my freedom and feel myself being lifted out of any feeling of dependency to a realm of serenity.

Enfolded in the peace of God, I am aware of God's presence within. I recognize that I am being transformed into a glorious expression of divine freedom.

I am one with God, and I embrace
my freedom now!

Day 252

◆

Leap, and the net will appear.
—Julie Cameron

DAY BY DAY   I have faith in God, and that faith is enough to get me through any challenge that may come my way. It is enough to keep me on a steady course as I follow the guidance God is constantly giving me.

I follow the divine guidance I receive by following the light—the light of God, which radiates from within me. I am God's love in expression, and it is through giving expression to love that my faith continues to grow.

With courage and certainty, each thought I think and each action I take can be one in which I experience the fullness of God's presence.

Because I have opened my heart to God's joy and peace, I realize that I have all the faith I need right now. Day by day, my faith is continually growing stronger and my love for God is becoming ever greater.

Each day, I meet every situation with faith.

Day 253

—◆—

Painful as it may be, a significant emotional event can be the catalyst for choosing a direction that serves us— and those around us—more effectively.—Eric Allenbaugh

WINGS OF SPIRIT

Being without the companionship of someone or letting go of a way of life can be very difficult—especially when someone or something holds a special place in my heart or in my memories. Yet sometimes it is only through letting go that I can open the way for new good to come to me.

So I let go and let God. I give thanks for the blessing that a person or job or some item has been to me in the past, and then I let it go. With all my heart, I know that God is in charge, that God is guiding me to the people and opportunities which will bless me now.

I release concerns and know that God is in charge of my life. Then I reach new heights of acceptance and understanding.

I am uplifted on the wings of Spirit as I let go and let God.

Day 254

—◆—

Call it a clan, call it a network, call it a tribe,
call it a family: Whatever you call it, whoever you are,
you need one.—Jane Howard

POWER OF PRAYER

I have been touched and inspired by the power of prayer in my life, so I naturally want to include others in my prayers. I envision my prayers reaching out to them, helping them through all difficulties:

"God, thank You for guiding and protecting those whom I cherish. In releasing concern about them, I know that the light of Your love is illuminating their lives and that the power of Your life is restoring them.

"I also remember the people of the world in my prayers. You are the source of peace and harmony that ends all disagreements and unites all nations. I pray that all citizens of the world experience the peace of mind and the healing that come from knowing Your presence."

Today and every day, I include others in my prayers.

Day 255

—◆—

Why, indeed, must "God" be a noun?
Why not a verb—the most active and dynamic of all?
—Mary Daly

INSPIRATION

In a time of confusion or crisis, I turn to God for direction in what to say or do. Oftentimes, when I am looking back on a situation, I am surprised that I was capable of expressing such great insight.

When I don't let my own limited thoughts get in the way, I naturally open a clear way for divine ideas to flow from me. Thoughts and ideas inspired by God then become a part of my conversations and my interactions with others.

God inspires me to be kind and considerate to others. Because everything I think, say, and do is inspired by God's spirit within me, I catch a glimpse of my own spirituality.

I know the pure joy of having followed through on divine inspiration.

God inspires me.

For the Children

Hello God,

I've heard grownups talk about the Golden Rule and I know that it says to treat other people nicely because that's the way I want them to treat me.

When I play with my friends, I try to be nice all the time. If somebody does not play fair with me or calls me names, I think about how You would want me to act and what You would do if You were in my shoes.

God, I've been practicing the Golden Rule, and I can tell that my friends, teachers, and family like it. I have even more friends than before, and all of them are really fun to be with!

I like me when I'm nice, and so does everybody else. The Golden Rule is true: When I'm nice to people, they are nice to me, too!

Day 257

—◆—

*It is from prayer that
the spirit's victory springs.*
—*Schillerbuch*

**I'M
READY**

I always want to be as ready as I can be for a job interview or a test—for any opportunity to do my best. And there are things I can do to get ready: I study and prepare, I remain confident in my abilities, and I remind myself that God is with me in every moment and in all circumstances.

Yet what prepares me most to deal with both challenge and opportunity is my quiet time in prayer with God. Prayer strengthens and renews me. I feel reconnected with my own spirituality and aware of my oneness with God.

So I make a commitment to pray. If I have a regular prayer time, that's great. If I don't, I can take prayer breaks during the day—just a few moments of quiet contemplation will help me get focused. Then I will be open to divine direction and ready for whatever the day may hold.

My quiet times with God prepare me for the day.

Day 258

—◆—

All who believed were together
and had all things in common.
—Acts 2:44

SUPPORTING GRACE

The grace of God is divine love in action. This divine energy that drives good moves throughout humanity from person to person, from one generation to the next, inspiring and blessing.

So I know that the grace of God works for me and through me and others. I feel the presence of grace supporting me in fulfilling my goals. I also understand that there are other individuals who, through their work and caring, help me—directly and indirectly.

And for those things that I may feel are left undone, I know there are new generations coming along who will use their unique talents and abilities for the good of all humanity. By the grace of God, we are helping each other and our world.

Through the grace of God, I reach out to help others
and to help the world.

Day 259

—◆—

Be patient with yourself. Self-growth is tender;
it's holy ground. There's no greater investment.
—Stephen R. Covey

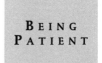

BEING PATIENT

The old adage that good things come to those who wait is a good reminder of the importance of being patient.

It's true: I find it is easy to be patient when things are going the way I want them to go. However, I want to remain calm even when my best plans go awry. I do when I remember that God is the creator and guiding force of all creation. Knowing and affirming this truth helps me to remain serene.

When I am calm and at peace within myself, I am more understanding of others. It seems so easy to be patient when I am calm. Most important, I understand that no failed plan can keep the blessings God has in store for me from coming to me. Oh, how good being patient feels to me!

I am patient and kind.

Day 260

—◆—

*A handful of pine-seed will cover mountains with the green
majesty of forests. I, too, will set my face to the wind
and throw my handful of seed on high.—Fiona Macleod*

**CELEBRATION
OF LOVE**

What joy I feel when I am able to
spend time with my loved ones! The
love in my heart goes out to them, and
I welcome the love they give to me.
We are truly one in the love we share with one another.

Even when we cannot be together physically, we are
united in a spirit of love that time and distance cannot
dim. We celebrate our togetherness when we
understand that our love is an expression of the spirit of
God within us.

Divine love flows through us all. No matter how far
we may be from each other, it is our spiritual
connection that unites us in a joy-filled celebration of
God's love. So whether we are spending time together
in person or connecting in heartfelt thought and prayer,
we share the love of God with one another.

**I join with family and friends in
a heartfelt celebration of divine love.**

Day 261

---◆---

At every moment, our bodies are continually responding to the messages from our minds. So what messages is your mind giving your body?—Margo Adair

HEALING POWER

God's mighty healing power is within me always. So if ever I need a healing—healing in my body, healing of emotions, healing in a relationship, or healing in the way I think—I call upon God. God answers, bringing healing to all areas of my life.

God is healing me now! As I speak these words, I visualize energizing, healing power filling every cell of my body. I feel a new strength building within me and have a renewed appreciation for the wonder that I am.

God loves me, and I have faith that God's love will heal my heart and help me with my relationships. I express God's love as forgiveness and then watch the wondrous healings that take place.

I have unshakable faith in God's healing power.

Day 262

—◆—

It's lack of faith that makes people afraid
of meeting challenges.
—Muhammad Ali

SWEET ASSURANCE Even though I know that divine order is always present and active in my life, I may sometimes hesitate to follow through on the guidance I receive. Yet whenever I want to move past such a hesitation, I can.

I gain new courage and strength when I affirm in silence or out loud: I am strong. God is with me and will never leave my side. With God to guide me and show me the way I should go, I can never fail.

God will never fail me. These heartwarming words reach to the core of my being and fill my soul with sweet assurance. I am able to take the first step in following divine guidance, knowing that the presence of God supports me every step of my way.

The sweet assurance of divine order
gives me courage.

Day 263

—◆—

When we choose not to focus on what is missing from our lives but are grateful for the abundance that's present . . . the wasteland of illusion falls away and we experience heaven on earth.—Sarah Ban Breathnach

WORLD OF WONDERS God, through laughter I hear what joy sounds like. As I watch the face of a person seeing a loved one for the first time in many years, I see what joy can look like.

When I behold the beauty You create in a sunrise that fills the horizon of the morning sky, I feel the joy of being one of Your wonders in this world of wonders. As I listen to Your wisdom and follow Your guidance, I am able to live that joy and express it to others through my own words and actions.

God, each day You give me a glimpse of the endless possibilities that You have provided for me. What joy I feel in knowing that the possibilities for joy are endless!

I hear, see, and feel the joy of God.

Day 264

—◆—

Forgiveness does not change the past,
but it does enlarge the future.
—Paul Boese

QUESTIONS OF THE HEART

How can I forgive the seemingly unforgivable? How do I get past the feeling of disappointment and hurt when I feel as though my trust in another person has been misplaced? I remember that the unconditional love of God is the key which will unlock the door to forgiveness.

When I choose not to fault others and instead focus on working toward a solution, I am doing myself a favor. By choosing God's way—the way of love and forgiveness—I am choosing to promote harmony and better relationships with the people in my family, school, workplace, and neighborhood.

I act in loving ways—even in what I perceive to be a negative situation—because I know from experience that positive actions promote positive reactions.

Love and forgiveness answer the questions
of my heart.

Day 265

---◆---

I am one of those who never knows the direction
of my journey until I have almost arrived.
—Anna Louise Strong

DIRECTING ME
A road map is a handy guide that indicates the way to many places. However, such a map is limited in the guidance it gives; it does not show me what to expect in the way of traffic, weather conditions, or detours.

On the other hand, God's guidance is unlimited—complete and whole—directing me around any obstacles in my way. I may not know exactly what lies ahead, but as I listen to the spirit of God within me, I will be safely guided.

Seeking divine guidance, I am not concerned about what might happen; I know that God will lead me throughout my journey in life. I can then relax and enjoy the beauty of the day and value each moment for the treasure that it is.

**With God as my guide, every day
is a great, new adventure.**

Day 266

---◆---

The awakening has begun!
—William Dempsey

SPIRIT OF HARMONY   Differences in outlooks, opinions, or beliefs may cause me to feel alienated from others—even my own family and friends. Yet there is something all-powerful that keeps my relationships with others healthy and whole: We share a unity of spirit.

The very spirit of God is within each person, and when I acknowledge the presence of God within myself and all other people, I bring love and harmony to all my relationships. The magnitude of our differences then fades away.

How much easier it is to live and work in harmony with others when I know their true identities as members with me in the family of God!

The spirit of God unites me in love and harmony with all people. I know this truth so completely that I live it in my life—every day and in every way.

**The spirit of God unites me in love
and harmony with all people.**

Day 267

◆

To insure good health: Eat lightly, breathe deeply,
live moderately, cultivate cheerfulness, and maintain
an interest in life.—William Londen

DIVINE
BALANCE
I have been taught from an early age to take care of my body by eating the right foods and getting plenty of exercise and rest. I enrich my mind by going to school, by reading, and by using what I learn in everyday living.

In order to truly thrive, however, I must also nourish my soul. I remain healthy when I maintain a divine balance in my life. I do this by spending time with God in prayer.

"God, You bless my soul and give me the spiritual, physical, and mental nourishment I need to live a healthy, well-balanced life.

"Your loving presence, God, nourishes me. Thank You for the spiritual feast that You set before me each day. Because of it, I am complete and whole."

God loves me and cares for me, nourishing
my soul and my life.

Day 268

—◆—

I am born happy every morning.
—Edith Wharton

MY HEART SINGS

Although no audible words may escape my lips, my heart sings with jubilation. I am alive and alert with the Spirit of life! A lightness of spirit is evident in me as radiant health and a positive nature.

My heart sings a song of life! The same kinds of atoms that give shape and substance to my body also give shape and substance to all creation.

My heart sings a song of joy and jubilation, for I am alive! The song of life I sing sounds something like this:

"Thank You, God, for allowing me to be a part of this life experience. You, dear God, are my sacred, eternal connection to all creation. Your life—divine life—fills me with hope and inspiration."

My heart sings a song of jubilation.

Day 269

—◆—

Try curiosity!
—Dorothy Parker

EXUBERANCE For a child, the world is a place filled with wonder. Watching the eyes of children open wide with amazement and seeing their fascination with new sights is an experience of joy for all.

I, too, can feel that same youthful exuberance and excitement for the wonders of God's world. When I consider the marvels of life that seem impossible, but that God makes possible, I am amazed. How could such small wings lift the oversized body of a bumblebee off the ground? Yet they do, and the bumblebee flies! How does a delicate plant find and then break through a tiny crack in an expanse of rock or cement? Yet it does!

In awe and wonder I say, "Thank You, God, for Your wonderful world!" God-life will always find a way to flourish and to be expressed.

Thank You, God, for Your wonderful world!

Day 270

— ◆ —

Trust yourself. Create the kind of self that you will
be happy to live with all your life. Make the most
of yourself by fanning the tiny, inner sparks of possibility
into flames of achievement.—Foster C. McClellan

CIRCLE OF LOVE
In order to feel loved, we need to express love. Our love is kept strong by mutual respect and concern for all in the circle of God's family.

As we turn to each other for support and encouragement, we open a door to better communication and a clearer understanding of the divine love that fills our lives.

The power of God is so strong in us that we are able to draw upon that strength to surpass any situation which might have otherwise limited us in some way. Yet this timeless divine power is gentle enough to guide us toward experiencing overwhelming love and compassion for all humankind. God is the strength that we need and the love that we so crave.

My Pillar of Faith
by Richard Maraj

I had never been so frightened. At age 19, I was being rushed to the hospital in an ambulance after being injured in an automobile accident.

It had happened so fast: Just after being thrown from the passenger seat, I was hit by the car. Covered with blood and in extreme pain, I knew I had been hurt, and my anxiety over just how badly I had been hurt grew with each passing minute during the ambulance ride.

Suddenly I was jarred out of my thoughts when the doors of the ambulance opened. Immediately I saw a familiar face waiting outside the emergency entrance to the hospital. Love took on visible form in that moment—in the face of my mother. Her love enfolded me, even before she reached my side and kissed my head. Without having to speak a word, she told me through her love and faith that everything would be okay.

Later, however, when I learned I was paralyzed from the waist down, I thought my life was over, at least the life I had known as an athlete—captain of the basketball team and city high-jump champion. I lost all faith—in God and in myself—but Mother's faith never wavered; she continued to love me and pray for me. Even seeing me at my worst—physically and emotionally—she never lost faith, never gave up on me.

One of my worst moments came when Mother was exercising my legs. She would lift and move my legs, doing for me what I could no longer do myself. Feeling such anger over my condition, I lashed out, yelling and thrashing my arms around in the air. I knocked over a lamp and a nearby basket of clothes. I hit the pillow, the wall, and then my head. She knew when to say something and when not to say anything. After I had finished venting, Mother calmly picked up the lamp and the clothes, tapped my leg and said, "Let's keep going," then started exercising my legs again.

I was tortured by not being able to walk, but I was even more tortured by thoughts of unforgiveness. The day I was injured, the young man driving the car had fallen asleep at the wheel and caused the crash. Neither he nor my girlfriend, who was sitting in the back, was injured. I hated him for what he had done to me. I took pleasure in revenge fantasies: how I could pay him back. That hate was crippling me more than the paralysis.

One day, I happened to pick up a little magazine my mother read every day. I knew *Daily Word* had helped her have faith, so I opened it to the message for that day. As I read, I had an overwhelming feeling that someone had written that message just for me. It was on forgiveness— how the person who forgives is always first to be blessed.

That message held a mirror up to me and said, "Brother, look at what you are doing to yourself." I understood that through forgiveness, I had the power to free myself from the hate that was ruining my life.

Forgiveness was the beginning of a new life for me. That new life has not been easy, but it is always meaningful. I'm a minister in that new life—driving, traveling by air, and walking—with the aid of braces and crutches.

I love and appreciate life now even more than I did before the accident. I love and appreciate my mom. No one has inspired or touched my life as she has. She has been my loving, constant pillar of faith. Through her, I came into the world. With her help, I was able to move from hatred to forgiveness, which opened the door to God. Mom provided the loving environment I needed to learn, and God worked wonders through that loving environment.

I have walked and not walked. I would love to walk alone, using my legs and giving my arms a rest, but I don't need that to happen. I'm not waiting for life to be perfect. I'm living and enjoying life now.

Day 271

—◆—

For your steadfast love is before my eyes,
and I walk in faithfulness to you.
—Psalms 26:3

MESSAGE OF HOPE Wherever they are or whatever they are doing, my loved ones are in my thoughts and prayers. Through gentle thoughts in sacred prayer times, God gives me a message of hope and assurance.

"Beloved, I have heard your prayers and understand how much you care about the ones you hold in prayer. Know that My loving presence is with them. They may not always be aware of Me, but I am aware of them. Every hour of the day or night, I am with them.

"I know their needs and concerns before they can even express them. As they go about their days, I am there to guide them safely through every circumstance. I am strength on which they can draw and comfort to which they can turn—anytime. Just as surely as I love and care for you, beloved, I also love and care for them."

As I pray for others, I affirm:
God loves and cares for you—always!

Day 272

—◆—

Your treasure house is within;
it contains all you'll ever need.
—Hui-Hai

G O D
I S   M Y
P E A C E

In my heart and mind, I know that God is with me as my peace in every circumstance. On occasion, however, my awareness of this truth may become overshadowed by the confusion or emotions I am experiencing.

If I am going through a stressful time, I need to have greater peace. So rather than focusing on why something has happened, I gain peace by turning within and allowing God's love to support me.

God strengthens me and helps me through any troubling time. As I turn to God for peace and assurance, I am gently reminded that I am never alone. I am enfolded in the love and care of God—now and forever.

God is the source of my inner peace as I make it through any change or challenge.

God, You are the source of my peace.

Day 273

—◆—

Faith is not contrary to reason.
—Sherwood Eddy

FLOURISHING LIFE

After a forest fire, the charred surface of land gives no clue to the activity of life underneath. Yet life is there, actively at work creating new growth. God has created all life, and life that God has created will find a way to flourish.

I am filled with life—divine life. God created me with the potential for healing and renewal. Like the new life under the surface of the ground, there is new life within me.

So if I appear on the surface to be less than a picture of health, I have faith that divine life is already doing a healing work within me. Where there is faith, there is also hope.

God is life, and the life of God is constantly healing and renewing me. I am a whole and healthy being.

**The life of God flows through me,
healing and renewing me.**

Day 274

—◆—

Only in growth, reform, and change,
paradoxically enough, is true security to be found.
—Anne Morrow Lindbergh

MY ANCHOR No matter how well I plan, a move to a new home, new school, or new environment can leave me feeling anxious. Or a sudden change may cause me to feel as if I have lost control—control of my life and of my reactions to what I am experiencing.

So at all times, I remind myself that God is my anchor through any storm, that God will keep me safe. In my times of prayer and meditation, I enter into a haven of peace—a space in time where I can relax for a moment and feel secure. I think of nothing else but being in God's peace-filled presence.

How good it is to know that God is always with me! What joy I feel in knowing that I am safe and secure— no matter what is going on in my life.

I am safe and secure in the presence of God.

Day 275

—◆—

*I believe, though I do not comprehend, and I hold
by faith what I cannot grasp with the mind.*
—Saint Bernard

**BUILDING
BLOCKS
OF FAITH**

There is no better way I could build faith than to have faith in God. My prayers are the building blocks to a greater faith, so I pray:

"God, I do have faith in You. When I am feeling down, I know that You are the strength which builds me up and the wisdom which opens a world of possibilities to me.

"My faith is growing; I feel sure that You are with me. New life is emerging in every cell of my body so that I am constantly being renewed. New hope rises to greet me each day as Your plan of divine order is unfolding.

"As my faith in Your spirit moving through me increases, so does the positive impact I have on my own life and on the lives of my loved ones.

"Yes, God, I have faith in You!"

**Each prayer I pray is a building block
in my growing faith.**

Day 276

— ◆ —

You can give without loving, but you
cannot love without giving.
—Amy Carmichael

SOMETHING GREATER

Here I am God! Guide me in doing what will bless and nurture people and help relieve their pain. Show me how I can be an instrument of Your love and caring.

Speak messages of hope and life through me, for I welcome the privilege of sharing Your love with others. In every moment that I let Your voice be my voice, I express words of love and compassion.

God, I have a purpose to fulfill as You guide me on the path of life. This is a path that leads me to something greater than I could ever have envisioned for myself.

Out of love and reverence for You, I do not miss any opportunity to share my faith in You with others. I am ready, willing, and able to follow Your guidance, dear God.

I welcome each new day with exuberance and joy,
for something greater is awaiting me.

Day 277

—◆—

*When you are doing the work you love, all else in life
seems to fall into place. . . . Your sense of personal worth
is keen, and you then see the personal worth of others.*
—Nancy Anderson

**WORK
OF LOVE**

Every activity of my life becomes a
work of love when I am dedicated to
working with God. I achieve this high
standard by being aware that I am
always in God's holy presence. God has given me all
the energy and understanding I need to bless what I do
with my own personal touch.

So whether I am busily at work in my home, at
school, or in the office, each task that comes my way is
one that I can be blessed by and give a blessing to.

Who knows how many people will be affected by
what I do? Working with God, my blessings travel like
ripples in the water, reaching out far and wide to others
in my family and in my community.

**Working with God, I create a life
that is a work of love.**

Day 278

— ◆ —

The foundations of a person are not
in matter but in spirit.
—Ralph Waldo Emerson

SPIRITUAL AWAKENING Each day I awaken not only physically but also spiritually. The stirring of Spirit within me alerts me to the unlimited potential that each moment holds. Then I know I am at the threshold of a new adventure in living.

What I do to start my day sets the tone for the whole day, so I awaken to my own spirituality—the presence of God within me—and to the sacredness of all creation—the presence of God everywhere.

A spiritual awakening is a renewing experience. Because I am fully conscious of God, I am alert to divine possibilities. Such a revelation may come about in a time of prayer or quiet reflection, but insight can come to my attention at any time—even when I am busily going about my day. So I stay alert and ready to act from the spirit of God within me!

Spiritually awake, I am aware of the presence
of God—everywhere.

Day 279

—◆—

It's the repetition of affirmations that leads to belief.
And once that belief becomes a deep conviction,
things begin to happen.—Claude M. Bristol

EXPECT TO BE BLESSED

Worry and stress are not new to life on Earth. Jesus encouraged people not to worry, giving them example after example of God's love and care for them. Jesus gently guided their expectation away from fear and toward God and the goodness of God.

What are my expectations for today? Because I know that God loves me and cares for me, I feel the assurance of my Creator with me now and at all times.

"God, I expect to be blessed by You, and I live in the joy of such expectation. What a relief it is not to worry about what could happen but, instead, to believe that there is a blessing for me no matter what happens. My expectations are built on the firm foundation of Your presence. Thank You, God, for blessing me."

**My expectations are built on
the firm foundation of God's presence.**

DAILY WORD FOR FAMILIES

Day 280

—◆—

Love is a force more formidable than any other. It is invisible . . . yet it is powerful enough to transform you in a moment and offer you more joy than any material possession could.—Barbara de Angelis

VOICE OF HARMONY AND LOVE I am constantly telling myself who I want to be—through my silent thoughts, spoken words, and secret hopes. So as I listen to what I am telling myself and others, I want to hear a voice of love and harmony.

Believing I can be is inherent to being God's love and harmony in expression. Then I encourage myself to be loving and kind. The love of God loves through me. The peace of God is expressed by me in all of my relationships and actions.

Does this mean that I will never have a thought or speak a word which is less than positive about myself or others? Maybe not; however, if I do, I let a language of love and harmony transform my attitude into a positive one.

I use a language of love and peace with myself and others.

Day 281

—◆—

Since you are like no other being ever created
since the beginning of time, you are incomparable.
—*Brenda Ueland*

RAINBOW EXPERIENCES A majestic rainbow arching brilliant colors across the sky is an inspiring sight. After a downpour of rain, a rainbow is a gentle reminder of the power of God to bring about change and transformation.

In my own life, I have rainbow experiences out of which challenges become unique opportunities for something better for me. So I look beyond appearances to the potential for good that is contained in every experience.

God has created me for life—so I live life fully. I follow the path that my Creator guides me to take. As I live each rainbow experience, I give thanks for it and for the opportunity to learn and grow from it.

In the midst of any challenge, there is
a fresh new opportunity for transformation,
and I am eager to discover it.

Day 282

—◆—

Faith is power to believe
and power to see.
—Prentice Mulford

HEALING FAITH God, the thoughts I think and the words I speak are extensions of my faith in You. So I choose thoughts and words that proclaim the presence of Your spirit within me. These are thoughts that soothe my mind and words that are a wake-up call for the healing of my body.

There is life within every cell of my body that responds to my thoughts and words of healing and renewal. I am healed because the life You created in me is renewing life.

God, thank You for giving me life and for renewing my life. I live fully and completely because I know that Your spirit is living out through me as health and vitality, enthusiasm and creativity. My faith in You sparks a healing response within me.

My thoughts and words of faith spark
a healing response within me.

Day 283

———◆———

There are some people who have the quality of richness and joy in them and they communicate it to everything they touch. It is first of all a physical quality; then it is a quality of the spirit.—Thomas Wolfe

JOY OF SPIRIT

A smile spreading across my face is an outer indication of a feeling of happiness. However, that feeling may be only temporary. True, absolute joy comes from the spirit of God within me. This joy causes my soul to smile continuously.

Because I am filled with the joy of Spirit, I smile with my eyes, also. Just thinking of the blessings that divine love brings to me causes my eyes to dance and twinkle with the warm glow of Spirit.

My inner joy is also evident in my loving words and thoughtful actions, which naturally come about because I know how good it feels to express joy. The way I share with and care about others is directly related to the joy of Spirit I feel.

True happiness comes from knowing that I am filled with the joy of Spirit.

Day 284

—◆—

The garden is growth and change and that means
loss as well as constant new treasures to make up
for a few disasters.—May Sarton

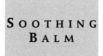

SOOTHING BALM

A healing balm eases the ache in overused or strained muscles. Even more profoundly, God's loving presence soothes me and restores peace to my mind and heart.

Despite what is happening around me, I can always turn to God for comfort and relief. God's loving presence is always with me, always ready to help me find my way. So if I am facing a loss—of a friend, a job, or even a bit of self-esteem—I give the situation to God and let God show me how to find peace.

God's steadfast love for me is the assurance of never-ending care and unlimited possibilities. So I understand that I never have to face any loss alone. God is my constant companion, showing me the way back into the sunlight of life.

God's loving presence is a soothing balm
that comforts and restores me.

Day 285

—◆—

*When you affirm your own rightness in the universe,
then you cooperate with others easily and automatically
as part of your own nature.—Jane Roberts*

**LIVING
MY
VISION**

I hold a vision in my mind's eye—
a picture of a world enveloped in a
golden glow. This glow is the light of
love—divine love that spans the globe
and eliminates all darkness.

The love of God is pure and unconditional and
cannot be confined or diminished. Love has the power
to turn strangers into friends, negatives into positives,
hurtful words into helpful ones.

The vision of a world of love can become a reality,
even if it is through the actions of one person at a time.
I do my part by being loving and open to everyone
around me.

At all times, I hold in mind a picture of a world aglow
with love—a world of hope and opportunity, a world of
peace and happiness for all people.

I do my part in shaping a world of love.

For the Children

Hello God,

My kitten has taught me something: Animals and people don't have to speak to understand each other. When my kitten waves her fluffy tail back and forth, she is letting me know that she is glad to see me. When she purrs, she is telling me that she loves me. And I'm sure that when I pet her, she knows I am really saying, "I love you, too!"

The way my kitten and I talk without having to say words reminds me of how You and I talk. It's as if we can feel each other's thoughts and words.

Sometimes I feel You whisper to me, telling me to look both ways before I cross the street. Or when I'm scared in my bed at night, You let me know that You are there with me.

I know You hear me, God, whether I am saying words or just thinking them. And that is really neat!

Day 287

$\bullet$

You don't need an explanation for everything. Recognize that there are such things as miracles—events for which there are no ready explanations. Later knowledge may explain those events quite easily.—Harry Browne

OPEN TO GUIDANCE If I were to ask several people what I should do about a challenge, I would probably get several different opinions. The sure way out of such confusion is to ask God for a solution. I do this by quietly turning my attention away from the challenge and toward the spirit of God within me.

Then I simply say, "God, guide me in doing what is mine to do." I remain quiet—not so much to receive an answer at that moment, but to be sure that the act of surrender, of turning it over to God, is complete.

I remain open to divine guidance at all times, knowing that it will indeed come to me. Then I recognize divine ideas and act on them.

God, You are my guide in doing what is mine to do.

Day 288

If we give love its proper expression,
our life unfolds like a beautiful flower.
—William L. Fischer

SPIRITUAL ROOTS

Plants need special care and nourishment in order to thrive and grow. Such attention almost guarantees that the result will be healthy plants with strong roots, which will support them for many years to come.

The same is true for me. I am an important member of God's universal family, and the love I receive from others is one way I am nourished. Such care feeds my soul and supports my spiritual development.

Yet what happens if I feel unloved? I remember that I have deep spiritual roots, for I am firmly grounded in the rich soil of God's everlasting love. Divine love provides the nourishment for every relationship I have or will ever experience. Sharing love with others, I help create an atmosphere of love.

I have deep spiritual roots, for I am firmly grounded in God's everlasting love.

Day 289

---◆---

*God's gifts put man's best dreams
to shame.*
—Elizabeth Barrett Browning

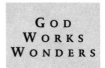
**GOD
WORKS
WONDERS**

Learning how to truly let go and let God work through me may seem to take a lifetime, and I'd like to know how right now. Yet through daily experiences of acting upon my faith in God, I do learn to let go of concern and let God do what is best.

Letting God do a divine work through me, I put aside any thought of limitation that might get in the way of a solution—no matter what the situation may be. I free my mind of fear, worry, and regret and know that in the process of letting go, I give my attention wholly to God.

Immediately I feel the positive results. Alert to divine wisdom, I cooperate with the divine work that God is bringing about.

I let go and let God work wonders through me.

Day 290

—◆—

Of all musical instruments the human voice
is the most beautiful, for it is made by God.
—Shusha Guppy

MELODY OF LIFE Becoming still for a moment, I do absolutely nothing else but be open to experiencing the presence of God. Then I hear God's beautiful melody of life, which is a message that stirs hope within me.

Here in the stillness, I retreat from the physical world and let my senses rest. Aware of my own spiritual nature, I touch the presence of God within me. Experiencing the presence of God so fully, I discover inner wisdom, strength, and peace.

God's beautiful melody of life is always playing through me and to me—through all life and to all life. I am thankful to be alive and to be experiencing life at this time. I have a greater appreciation for life and notice the magnificence and beauty that are in all life—from the smallest to the largest forms. Thank God for life!

Thank You, God, for the beautiful melody
of life playing through me.

Day 291

—◆—

I believe that dreams are more powerful than facts—
that hope always triumphs over experience.
—Robert Fulghum

INSPIRED BY GOD

The success of any project usually rests in the hands and hearts of the ones who have caught sight of a divine idea and put all their efforts into making that idea a reality. Inspired by God, they have unwavering belief in themselves, in what they are doing, and in all who are working toward making that goal a reality.

My success in all matters is strengthened by my dedication to keeping my goals clearly in mind and heart. Because my dreams are inspired by God, the spirit of God within gives me the courage to keep on keeping on while guiding me successfully through and around every challenge.

God's presence motivates me to do the most with my talents and abilities in order to reach the fulfillment of my dreams.

My goals are dreams that are inspired
by God and becoming reality.

Day 292

—◆—

Nothing liberates our greatness like
the desire to help, the desire to serve.
—Marianne Williamson

GIFT OF LOVE

I may devote a lot of time to finding that perfect gift for a birthday celebration or some other special occasion. Yet it is often not the gift itself but the loving thought behind it that means the most to the one who receives it.

The love and affection shared in those special moments of giving and receiving create treasured memories, for they establish a heart connection that lasts through the most challenging of times.

Best of all, I don't have to wait for a special occasion to give a gift; I can give the gift of myself every day. The gift of my undivided attention, the smile that is uniquely my own, the nod of encouragement to a friend are all gifts that I can give. Through sharing the gift of love, I am sharing a bit of God with the world.

I give the gift of myself—my love
and encouragement—every day.

Day 293

—◆—

It is by forgiving
that one is forgiven.
—Mother Teresa

HEALING THROUGH FORGIVENESS Forgiving others when they act as if they don't care how their words or actions have affected me may not be easy. Nonetheless, I can and do forgive because God's unconditional love is living in me and through me.

I recognize that we are all children of God and, therefore, enfolded in the tender care of our Creator. I trust God to bring about what is right through me and through others. I welcome the wisdom from God that enables me to see each person in the light of understanding and acceptance.

Yes, other people may have done or said things that had the potential to hurt me, but God's love always heals me. As an open channel of God's love, I do forgive, which heals me and my relationships.

When I forgive, I encourage healing
of myself and my relationships.

Day 294

Let the little children come to me, and do not stop them;
for it is to such as these that the kingdom of heaven belongs.
—Matthew 19:14

AN INVESTMENT
Financial investments can mean greater financial stability for me and my family in the future. However, it is from my investments of love and kindness that I reap the richest rewards.

I make an investment in divine love by forgiving myself and others and moving on with my life. Because I fill my mind with loving thoughts, I take positive actions.

I invest in the future of the world by being a mentor to children. As I listen to divine guidance, I lead by example. By being an example of God's wonder in expression, I bring out the best in children.

I make an investment in the environment by acting responsibly when I am outdoors, for my interactions with all God's creatures and creations are based on care and consideration.

My positive actions are an investment in love.

Day 295

---◆---

As your hands and feet are parts of you,
so are the qualities of God woven into your being.
—Russel W. Lake

SACRED PARTNERSHIP

How easy it is to *say* that God is always with me, but how do I *know*—in the depths of my soul—that God is taking an active part in the story of my life?

I am sure that God and I form a sacred partnership because I can feel God's loving presence within me. That feeling springs forth from my faith. My faith in God fills me with an inner knowing that God loves me and will never fail me.

How magnificent God's grace is! I am filled with awe when I think about what grace means to me: I do not have to earn God's love by changing or becoming someone different. Grace is God's love for me and acceptance of me as I am right now.

God's grace blesses me with love and acceptance.

Day 296

---◆---

*Meditating upon it daily, you will
find your freedom.*
—Mary L. Kupferle

**CALL
TO
FREEDOM**
The call to freedom echoes
resoundingly in my mind and heart,
yet the definition of freedom is as
unique as each individual on the
planet Earth.

Regardless of how I or others may define freedom, it
is freedom of Spirit that affects me most profoundly.
This is the freedom that defines who I am as a member
of the family of God.

There is one family, united under God, and all
members are created to be free! Through my spiritual
freedom, I am able to break the bonds of mental or
physical stress in order to reach the mountaintop
experiences of life.

I am free! Praise God, I am free! I am being
transformed even now into a greater degree of spiritual
freedom.

I am free! Praise God, I am free!

Day 297

———◆———

*A healthful hunger for a great idea is
the beauty and blessedness of life.*
—Jean Ingelow

**CLEAR
INSIGHT**

At times I may catch a glimpse of a goal or an accomplishment that causes a surge of joy within me. Then, for some unknown reason, that dream evaporates.

However, I do not give up. With time, I will have much clearer insight and another chance in a relationship or for a career. In that in-between time—a time of faith and prayer—I have matured and so have the others involved.

Within every challenge or triumph, the glory of God is there with me, giving me another chance and clearer insight. I am a new creation in God with a confidence based on my faith in God.

**God is continually giving me another chance
and clearer insight.**

Day 298

—◆—

I have learned that to have a good friend is the greatest
of God's gifts, for it is a love that has no exchange
for payment.—Fannie Farmer

CHERISHED MEMORIES

When I think about the past, certain memories come to mind—especially those of the people and events that had an impact on how I view the world and that helped shape me into who I am today. I give thanks for these cherished memories and the joy they bring into my life—even now.

However, each moment of my life is an opportunity to create new memories. Yes, I have wonderful memories from the past, but I also look forward to the new and exciting adventures that God has in store for me. I savor the rich experiences that are a part of my life every day.

Because my attitude is one of anticipating more good from God, each day becomes a magical time that I can add to my storehouse of cherished memories.

I give thanks for cherished memories
and look forward to new adventures.

Day 299

—◆—

*In between goals is a thing called life
that has to be lived and enjoyed.*
—*Sid Caesar*

PURPOSE

More than likely, I have wondered about the meaning of life. What is my purpose and where will events lead me?

Although I may never have all the answers, there is one thing I can know for certain: There is meaning and purpose in every moment of life.

I am a beloved child of God, created for a divine purpose that only I can fulfill. While I may not always know what that purpose is, I can be sure that my existence makes the world a far better place.

This is all the reason I need to live life fully, to find meaning and purpose. I know this truth about myself and all others.

**I embrace the meaning and purpose
in every moment of life.**

Day 300

Circle of Love

Living and working and playing with those we love is not always easy. We may be distracted by challenges and even crises that, as we focus on them, break our circle of love and cause us to drift apart.

Yet when we spend quiet, prayerful times together with family and friends, we build a powerful unity of spirit. Turning off the TV and radio, we may just sit quietly in the same room. In the quietness we acknowledge the presence of God within each other. We know that what each one of us loves about the others is far more than physical appearances and personalities.

We love God, and we love the people God has created to share life and love and joy with us. As we live and love from the presence of God within us, we form a sacred circle of love. The fullness of our love is expanded by each person who becomes a link in our circle of love.

We cannot love God without loving each other,
for humanity is of God and God is in humanity.
—Sue Sikking

MOMMA'S KISS
BY COLLEEN ZUCK

I n all my 37 years, I could not remember having felt so miserable. I had the flu, and each time I shuddered with the chills, my whole aching body seemed to ache even more. Not wanting to wake my husband, who was sleeping beside me, but not having the courage to leave the warm cocoon of my blankets, I tried to lie as still as possible.

Without my wanting it to happen, I let out a heavy sigh that woke Bill, and in a sympathetic voice he asked, "Honey, is there anything I can get you?" I'm sure he expected my request to be a couple of aspirins and a glass of water; however, I surprised myself as much as him when I answered, "I want my mommy!"

We both began to laugh at the thought of a grown woman wanting her mommy, and after I laughed I felt a little less miserable. I felt even better when I let memories of my mother fill my mind. Throughout my growing-up years, her kiss had eased both my emotional and physical hurts.

She had always been there for me whenever I needed her, doing everything she could think of to make me feel better. I imagined that my mother's prayers for me when I was sick went something like this: "God, I know You will heal her, and I'm going to do everything I can to help."

Sometimes her remedies were more unpleasant than whatever discomfort they were applied to. The mustard plasters, potato poultices, and herb teas she prepared were remedies that had been passed down through generations of her family. These were proven remedies they found helpful in surviving in the isolated hills of Madison County, Arkansas. Momma's nightly ritual with me was to always put me to bed and pray with me. Her kiss on my forehead was a signal that it was time for me to go to sleep.

Thinking of her kiss on the night I had the flu, I prayed, "God, if Momma would kiss my forehead right now, I know I would feel better and I would be able to sleep." I was beginning to chastise myself for such a childish prayer, when I felt the softest touch on my forehead.

Did Momma kiss me good night? With all my heart, I wanted to believe that she had. So I did believe. The more I let myself believe, the more sleepy I got, and soon I drifted off to sleep.

Time has changed us—both Momma and me. She was diagnosed with Alzheimer's disease several years ago. We children took care of her as long as possible, but her nights turned into times of anxious activity, preparing to go to her home "upon the hill in Arkansas."

Momma is in a special care unit now, near my work and home so I can visit her every day. I love to hug and kiss her—my attempt to keep her from slipping farther away from me. In her mind, she is moving back to the hills of Arkansas more and more. She takes her clothes out of her closet most days, and I put them back in the evening. Still, Momma knows the joy of living; her laughter bubbles up throughout the day and helps lift the spirits of everyone around her.

Nights are still difficult for Momma, and when I go to bed at night and say my prayers, I ask God to send her a kiss to help her sleep. She's never told me that when she's unable to sleep, she feels a gentle touch on her forehead—a kiss that soothes her anxiety and helps her drift off to much needed sleep.

With all my heart, I want to believe that my kiss does reach her. I do know that believing it helps *me* to sleep.

Day 301

—◆—

It helps, I think, to consider ourselves on a very long journey: the main thing is to keep to the faith, to endure, to help each other when we stumble or tire, to weep and press on.—Mary Caroline Richards

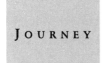

JOURNEY

Every day is a new beginning, and each beginning is the start of a grand and glorious adventure, a journey of the soul that awakens me to God.

I know that whatever happens today, God is with me. I can never be separated from the presence of God. Each day I move forward in greater understanding of my oneness with God.

The journey itself brings many rewards. Each moment is ripe with the potential to learn more about myself and others and to be the child of God I was created to be.

I learn more about God by becoming more loving and kind. My spiritual journey allows me to explore the meaning and purpose of my existence, and what I discover is my heart-and-soul connection with God.

**I am on a journey that brings me to
a greater awareness of God each day.**

Day 302

—◆—

*The nature of God is a circle of which the center
is everywhere and the circumference is nowhere.*
—Empedocles

**HEALING
PRESENCE**

When I need a healing, I pray. I pray remembering that within the physical body that gives me shape and substance is a divine presence—the spirit of God at the center of my being. I do all that I can to cooperate with the healing activity of God at this time and at all times.

Closing my eyes and letting my thoughts move from symptoms and pain to the presence of God within me stimulates the very cells of my body with healing.

I envision a powerful, healing light shining within my heart. As that light moves throughout my body, it cleanses my circulatory system and soothes my joints and muscles. Aglow with God's presence, I am healed and refreshed. Great joy rises from the depths of my soul to confirm my healing.

The presence of God heals and refreshes me.

Day 303

—◆—

*Joy is what happens to us when we allow ourselves
to recognize how good things really are.*
—*Marianne Williamson*

GOLDEN MOMENTS   With great pleasure, I may recall a time when all the pieces in the "puzzle" of my life seemed magically to fall into place. What joy I experienced when everything went smoothly and efficiently! Yes, that was truly a golden moment!

I can experience such joy in every moment when I invite God to think through me and to act through me. Then every moment is touched with the golden glow of God's spirit as it reaches out through me to bless each person and event.

What a relief to know that God is always with me! How grateful I am for each golden moment, each opportunity to let God's presence shine out from me to others!

**Each moment is a golden opportunity
to let God's presence shine from me.**

Day 304

— ◆ —

When they call to me, I will answer them;
I will be with them in trouble,
I will rescue them and honor them.
—Psalms 91:15

ANSWERED PRAYER

Whatever I need or desire, God will help me find the fulfillment I seek. God answers my every prayer, for God is the answer to prayer:

"Whenever you need Me, I am here for you. No dream is too great, no need so small that I cannot help you find the right solution.

"Trust in Me, beloved, and I will show you how to achieve more than you ever dreamed you could. I will take you beyond your grandest dream and show you a way that will bring untold blessings into your life.

"Whenever you call for Me, I will answer. Do not be confused if the answer you receive is not the one you expected. Know that because I love you, My answer will always be what is highest and best for you."

God, You are the answer to my every prayer.

Day 305

—◆—

The greatest pleasure in life is doing
what people say you cannot do.
—Walter Bagehot

ABILITIES

If I ever doubt my ability to succeed at something new, I need to remind myself that I am a capable, strong person. My reassurance comes from God—perhaps as the gentle nudge of encouragement I need to try new adventures and discover more about all that I can do.

Before I begin new projects, learn a new sport, or follow through on new opportunities, I take a moment to thank God for the abilities that I have and for those I have yet to discover.

I can succeed in accomplishing my heart's desire. In addition to my God-given talents and abilities, I have divine understanding that guides me in using them. Because God is continually encouraging me to achieve, I have confidence in myself and in the perfect outcome.

I thank God for the abilities I know I have and for the ones I have yet to discover.

Day 306

— ◆ —

I pray hard, work hard,
and leave the rest to God.
—Florence Griffith Joyner

RELY ON GOD

Letting go and letting God is a sacred activity of practicing my faith: I stop spending time worrying about someone or something and rely on God for guidance and the answer to prayer.

Letting go and letting God is also a practical approach to everyday life. What good does it ever do to worry? None whatsoever! So I let go of worry. Is there anything that cannot be accomplished by God? Of course not! So I let God be God in my life and in all that concerns me and my loved ones.

As I let go and rely on God, I am proclaiming my faith in God. With that trust, I have peace of mind. I think clearly, and I am ready to do my part in bringing about God's divine plan.

By letting go and relying on God,
I am proclaiming my faith in God.

Day 307

---◆---

What is life? It is the flash of a firefly in the night. It is the breath of a buffalo in the wintertime. It is the little shadow that runs across the grass and loses itself in the sunset.
—*Crowfoot, Blackfoot tribe*

SOURCE OF LIFE

Who and what are important in my life? Family and friends are probably at the top of my list, followed by a comfortable home, adequate clothing, and nourishing food. All this is vital to my health, yet even more important to my well-being is the life of God within me.

The spirit of God beats within my heart in a rhythm of love and peace. With every breath I take, divine life flows through me to energize the cells and tissues of every muscle and organ.

I could go for a period of time without food or water, friends or shelter. However, I could not go on for even a moment without the life of God within, which is constantly breathing through me, healing me, and energizing me.

> God is my source of life and my source
> for living a rich and fulfilling life.

Day 308

——◆——

We can build an awareness of God in the early morning that will carry us through the day. We can so unify ourselves with God at night that even in sleep we are awake to God.—Martha Smock

GOD SPEAKS TO ME

I turn to God in the stillness of my soul and listen as God speaks to me. Gently, lovingly, God's sweet message of assurance washes over me, whispering a message of love and peace:

"Beloved, call on Me in your times of need, and I will comfort you. Trust in Me with all your heart, and I will give you the courage to face any challenge.

"Whatever is before you, know that I am with you as you step out in faith. I love you unconditionally, and as you open yourself to My love, you will discover a peace that refreshes and heals you."

Divine peace fills my heart and gives me the courage to face any challenge.

Day 309

—◆—

In a way winter is the real spring, the time
when the inner things happen, the resurge of nature.
—*Edna O'Brien*

SACRED REALITY

The real me is so much more than my physical image or the way I sound. The authentic me is spiritual in nature and made in the image of God. So my identity as a spiritual being is what I keep in mind as I go about the day.

If ever I hear words coming from me that are less than kind or statements that are less than positive, I know to take a reality check. The real me is kind to others and trusts in God. The real me knows that thoughts and words are powerful, so I think and speak from my heart.

I experience such joy in being true to the spirit of God in me! Living in an awareness of God brings a divine authenticity to whatever I do.

I am an authentic spiritual being
living my sacred reality.

Day 310

—◆—

*True forgiveness, perhaps the only kind of forgiveness,
is self-forgiveness. God forgives as you forget and forgive,
as you rise above the limited consciousness and walk on.*
—*Eric Butterworth*

**OPEN
TO
HEALING**

Whether I desire a healing in my body or a relationship, I strive to be free of any thoughts or beliefs that might be slowing down or interfering with a healing.

Believing I deserve the greater blessings God has in store for me and expecting a healing to take place seem to speed up the healing process. So I put aside any thoughts or feelings that could come between me and my healing. I pave the way for answered prayer by forgiving myself and then letting God do the rest.

As I forgive, I invite God's healing activity into my mind and heart. Barriers of negativity are broken down so that the free flow of love and appreciation moves out from me to others. I accept the loving relationships and health that are mine to enjoy.

**As I forgive, I open the way to a healing of mind,
body, and emotion.**

Day 311

—◆—

Great music is in a sense serene;
it is certain of the values it asserts.
—Dame Rebecca West

TRUE GREATNESS Jesus asked a child to come forward as an example of greatness when His disciples asked, "Who is the greatest in the kingdom of heaven?" (Matthew 18:1–2)

Surely there is a greatness within children that allows them to love with a purity of heart and soul, which helps them to discover the wonder of life in even the smallest creeping bug. That greatness is within me and all people, because such greatness is from the presence of God, which lives within us all.

I experience true greatness whenever I put aside my ego and let the love of God be expressed by me. How great God is! How great I feel when I let the wonder of God be expressed by me and as me.

**As a humble child of God, I experience
true greatness!**

Day 312

—◆—

The only way to discover the limits of the possible
is to go beyond them into the impossible.
—*Arthur C. Clarke*

SPIRITUAL EXPLORER Throughout the centuries, explorers have discovered many incredible wonders in the world. I, too, am an explorer in my own right, for each day is a day in which I continue my quest to discover more of the wonder in life and what I am capable of achieving in my life.

Just as surely as every great explorer felt the excitement and thrill of discovery, I am filled with exhilaration. I am confident, too, for no matter where my journey may take me, God will be with me through it all.

I continue my discovery of my spiritual self by turning within and appreciating the sacredness I find there. In my times of prayer and meditation, God speaks to me and I am free to ask the questions of my heart and listen to divine answers.

I am discovering more of the magnificence
of God in me and in the world.

Day 313

— ♦ —

And God is able to provide you with every blessing
in abundance, so that by always having enough of
everything, you may share abundantly in every good work.
—2 Corinthians 9:8

GOD PROVIDES

How much is enough financially?
The answer to that question changes
with time and circumstance. For
instance, the average earnings of a
family 30 years ago would probably not support my
family or any other family today.

Yet because I know that God is the one source of all
blessings—whether material, spiritual, or otherwise—I
also know that God is enough for me:

"God, knowing that You are my provider opens a
world of opportunity to me. You help me to recognize
what would be a better career move and how to
enhance my relationships. Because I am aware of You, I
accept each opportunity and move with it. Thank You,
God, for blessing me!"

Knowing that God is my provider opens
a world of opportunity to me.

Day 314

—◆—

Differences challenge assumptions.
—Anne Wilson Schaefer

EMISSARY OF GOD'S LOVE
The people of the world are a diverse medley of individuals and represent many different cultures. I honor the diversity of all people as I follow God's guidance in expressing love and then living in the light of divine love.

It's true: The people who are sitting beside me at school or on a bus, working with me in the office, or living next door to me in my neighborhood may enjoy different lifestyles and traditions than I do. Wherever I am, though, I can help create an environment of understanding in which mutual respect and friendships are nurtured.

As I listen to and watch others, I learn more of the diverse wonders in a world of God's creation. With such understanding in my heart, I am an emissary of God's love.

I honor God and the diversity of God's creativity when I honor all people.

Day 315

—◆—

Faith is to believe what you do not see; the reward
of this faith is to see what you believe.
—Saint Augustine

IT'S POSSIBLE! Have I ever given up on some dream simply because it seemed impossible for me to achieve? Well, I know from this moment on that what may seem impossible for me alone is entirely possible when I include God in my plans and activities.

Jesus said, "For God all things are possible." (Mark 10:27) Not just some things, but *all* things are possible when I have faith that God will inspire me in choosing my goals and also help me in achieving them.

I would never dream if God did not inspire me to stretch and reach out beyond the limited expectations of myself and others. Every desire that can become a blessing comes from God. God not only gives me the dream but also shows me the way my dream can become a reality.

With God, all things are possible.

Day 316

For the Children

Hello God,

I don't really have anything to ask about today, but I did want to tell You how much I love You. You have given me so many neat things, and I just wanted to say "thank You!"

You gave me the best mom and dad, and my grandma and grandpa are special, too! And my friends are the greatest! We are all so different, but that is what makes it so fun to be around them! We don't always agree on everything, but something tells me that this is Your way of showing me how important we all are, no matter how different we may seem to be.

Well, I have to go now, God, but I want You to know that I am glad that You're my special friend.

Day 317

—◆—

Service is the rent we pay for being. It is the very purpose
of life, and not something you do in your spare time.
—Marian Wright Edelman

CARING FOR OTHERS   Perhaps there is no other role in life in which so much is asked of a person and so much is given in return than that of a caregiver. Being the eyes for those who are unable to see, the legs for those who are unable to walk, the voice for those who are unable to speak is truly being an expression of God in the world.

The helping hand, the words of encouragement, the loving touch that I offer to others move out from me as waves of blessings. As I bless others, I feel a surge of the power and love, the wisdom and patience of God moving in and through me.

I acknowledge the sacredness of each person, the wonder of each creature that God has created. Being a caregiver is a way of saying, "Thank You, God, for all precious life!"

My love for others is reflected in the way
I care for and about them.

Day 318

—◆—

We can only learn
to love by loving.
—Iris Murdoch

SONG OF HARMONY
My greatest desire is to be a loving expression of God's spirit in the world, and I thank God for showing me how to be more understanding of and caring toward others.

God has blessed me with peace, and I live from the peace of God within me. As an ambassador of God's love, I will do all that I can to promote harmony and peace within my own family and community.

God shows me the way to a greater awareness of the divine harmony and order that are inherent in all creation. As I become more aware of God's loving presence within me, my family, my friends, and my co-workers, I live a life of harmony.

I understand that God's love is in all people and can be expressed by all people.

My heart sings a song of harmony and love.

Day 319

—◆—

Sometimes the heart sees
what is invisible to the eye.
—H. Jackson Brown Jr.

CLEAR VISION

The picture I hold in my mind of how a situation may be resolved or what a loved one could choose to do may not be according to a divine plan. So rather than trying to take on the challenges of life by deciding how things *should* be, I remain flexible and open to God's way.

Daily prayer keeps my vision clear so that I am able to recognize the order of God's plan. The reality of my world is that God is in charge, and I make a conscious choice to relax and follow the guidance I receive.

Recognizing that God is in charge, I am relieved of tension and stress. Now I have such a clear vision that I am able to identify the divine plan that is unfolding. Knowing that it is something that contains a blessing, I am eager to cooperate with it.

As I release all concerns, I understand with clarity that God is in charge.

Day 320

———◆———

People are just about as happy as they
make up their minds to be.
—Abraham Lincoln

HERITAGE OF JOY
Joy is more than a feeling of gladness in response to certain people or events. Joy is my heritage as God's creation, for God created me to be a joy-filled person.

I am filled with the joy of living! When I wake in the morning, I give thanks for the new opportunities that await me.

I am filled with the joy of loving! I greet family and friends with love. I appreciate them as my loved ones and as God's beloved creations.

I am filled with the joy of giving! Each day I dedicate a portion of my time and energy to helping others in whatever way I can. Speaking kind words and acting in loving ways are simple but powerful ways of spreading joy.

It is my heritage to be a joy-filled person!

Day 321

—◆—

Life is the first gift, love is the second,
and understanding is the third.
—*Marge Piercy*

MY STORY Whether or not I capture it by pen or computer, I am writing my life story every day. I am thinking thoughts, making decisions, and taking actions that create the story of my life.

I remember Jesus' encouragement: "For everyone who asks receives, and everyone who searches finds, and for everyone who knocks, the door will be opened." (Matthew 7:8) I ask and search and knock by going to God in prayer.

I want my story to be about a person of faith. So I call on the spirit of God to live through me as love, understanding, and all the other qualities of a spiritually enlivened being.

In every situation, I seek divine guidance by asking, "What would God do?" The resounding answer I receive is this: "Be a blessing."

Every day is a new chapter in the story of my life.

Day 322

—◆—

Man is free at the moment
he wishes to be.
—Voltaire

FREE TO BE

What is it that I want to be free *from* today? Is it some negative habit or tendency? Is it the memory of a disturbing event that even now seems to upset me? Well, right now, I claim my freedom from it!

What is it that I want to be free *to do* today? Do I want to enjoy life and the people I share life with more than I ever have in the past? Do I want a more fulfilling job? Right now, at this very moment, I claim my freedom to do what is in my heart to do!

Where does the freedom from something and the freedom to do something come from? The source of my freedom is the spirit of God within me. I dare to claim my freedom because God has created me to be free—free from upset and pain and free to do all that enriches my soul and my life.

**God within me is my freedom, and I claim
my freedom now!**

Day 323

—◆—

I want, by understanding myself,
to understand others.
—Katherine Mansfield

LIGHT OF GOD

A theater spotlight is used to focus the attention of the audience on a particular player or part of the stage. By following the spotlight, the audience focuses on what is most important and comes away with a greater understanding of what they have seen and heard.

I gain greater understanding of any situation by putting it in the light—God's light. Like the spotlight in a play, the light of God takes my mind off distractions and focuses my attention on what I need to know. With God's help, I know that the words I speak and the actions I take are wise and compassionate.

The guidance of God is a light of love and understanding shining on the people and events that are an important part of my life.

I am guided by God's radiant light of love
and understanding.

Day 324

—◆—

The thing always happens that you really believe in;
and the belief in a thing makes it happen.
—Frank Lloyd Wright

UPLIFTING FAITH

Faith in God blesses me, for it gives me the understanding that I am surrounded by the power and presence of God at all times and in all places.

In my quiet times of prayer and meditation, I confide in God any concerns I may have. Then I release all to God for a divine solution.

As I pray, I can feel my faith in God uplift me. My prayers serve as reminders to me of the soul connection I share with God. Because I am one with God, I am one with pure, unconditional love and peace.

Even the most challenging difficulty is no cause for alarm. Faith is believing that divine power is supreme, and I do believe. I have faith that God strengthens, guides, and supports me in all that I do.

My faith uplifts me.

Day 325

---◆---

If you have made mistakes . . . there is always another chance for you. . . . You may have a fresh start any moment you choose, for this thing we call "failure" is not the falling down, but the staying down.—Mary Pickford

FRESH START

No matter how much I want it to happen or how hard I try to make it happen, I can never remain exactly the same from one day to the next. I take new thoughts, experiences, insights, and revelations with me into each new day, some of which affect me slightly and others which affect me profoundly.

So every day is a fresh start for me. Concerning my family, my job, my education—I put any thought of limitation or frustration in the past where it belongs! The wonderful news is this: God is within me and God is within all others. God is within every situation, helping me and helping others to make a fresh start in life, in a goal, or in a relationship.

This is a new day and a fresh start for me.

Day 326

—◆—

To understand the heart and mind of a person,
look not at what he has already achieved, but at
what he aspires to.—Kahlil Gibran

THEME SONG Even in the midst of what seems to be a chaotic situation, I can remain a peaceful center of calm. I can because I know that no matter what is happening around me, God is right there with me. Where God is, divine order will prevail.

So no matter how hectic my schedule becomes, I relax and open my mind to all the possibilities that each moment contains. Then I discover that even the events that are unplanned or unexpected can bless me with new understanding and appreciation.

Divine order, not disorder, is the theme song of my life. Affirming the truth of divine order opens my eyes to the beauty in everyone and everything around me. With new understanding, I appreciate the fact that even unexpected changes and challenges are a part of God's plan of divine order.

Divine order is the theme song of my life.

Day 327

—◆—

*I may not be totally perfect,
but parts of me are excellent.
—Ashleigh Brilliant*

AMAZING CREATION

Have I ever thought about just how amazing I am? From the top of my head to the tips of my toes, I am a magnificent creation—one of God's great masterpieces!

There is no other person in the world who can give to the world what I have to give. I have my own individual purpose in life, my own particular talents, for I am truly unique!

Now I consider the world around me. How wonderful is the planet I call home! How truly blessed I am to live in an environment that was created to sustain and nurture me and a world of other people.

Each day brings me a greater awareness of my oneness with God and a greater awareness of how amazing life is!

**I am one of God's amazing creations,
living in an amazing world.**

Day 328

—◆—

Laughter is by definition healthy.
—Doris Lessing

SENSE OF HUMOR Laughter is a form of healing therapy. A hearty laugh helps to stimulate the release of endorphins, a natural substance within my body that eases physical pain. When I laugh, my attention is shifted off health challenges and onto positive, lighthearted thoughts that promote healing.

Just thinking about a humorous event can invigorate me physically. As I laugh, I take in air and fill my lungs with oxygen which, in turn, rejuvenates the lifeblood of my body.

I feel so good when I laugh, and I share this invigorating experience with others by telling a humorous story. Laughter is even more enjoyable when it is shared with others, and I am enriched by the joy and laughter God has given to me.

**God has blessed me with
a healing sense of humor.**

Day 329

—◆—

*Always look for the sunlight
the Lord sends unto your days.*
—*Hope Campbell*

LOVING PRESENCE

I may not always feel comfortable in my surroundings, especially when I am traveling to or working in new areas. Yet even when I am away from familiar surroundings, I know that I am enfolded in the grace of God, which is the very love of God in expression.

With every step I take, my footsteps fall where the presence of God has already gone before me. So as I step forward, I do so with confidence and faith.

I am reassured by the understanding that God is protecting my loved ones, too. Even if I am not physically able to be with them, my mind is at ease, for I have faith in God to guide their way and keep them safe. My loved ones and I may be miles apart, but we are united in the oneness of God, a oneness of spirit.

**God's loving presence is within me
and my loved ones.**

Day 330

---◆---

Circle of Love

God created each and every one of us with such loving care, and it is only natural that we express love. From the love of God within us, we speak words and act in ways that maintain harmony and love in our relationships and in our environment.

While we know the importance of maintaining the balance in our spiritual, physical, and emotional lives, we can only achieve a true balance when we recognize the importance of each and every member of God's universal family.

Each of God's creations has a sacred purpose to fulfill, and we can be a positive influence on that fulfillment by encouraging and supporting one another as we grow through the experiences of our lives. With love in our hearts, we join together with family and friends to bring more love into the world.

I know why families were created, with all their imperfections. They humanize you. They are made to make you forget yourself occasionally, so that the beautiful balance of life is not destroyed.
—Anaïs Nin

SWEET MYSTERIES OF LIFE
BY EMANUEL CLEAVER

O ne of the sweet mysteries of life is that the most challenging times can also be the most fulfilling. When I reflect on the first seven years of my life—what my family did not have—it seems strange that it was such a happy time for me.

We lived in the small community of Waxahachie, Texas, in what at one time had been a slave shanty. There was no running water, no electricity, and no indoor plumbing. My father ran his own cleaners and did other work on the side. My mother was a housekeeper and took care of my three sisters and me.

All of us, parents and children, picked cotton, pecans, and peaches. We chopped cotton, harvested corn, and did whatever we could to generate money for the family. To be sure, we lived in what would be considered abject poverty today, but as far as I can remember, I was never hungry or without the clothes I needed.

What we did have was love and faith and a sense of the importance of family. But most important of all, we had an awareness of God. When I became extremely ill at the age of five, all these wonderful attributes supported me.

The attending physician did not think I could live for

more than six months. He put me on a restricted diet that was supposed to help keep me alive longer—if I adhered to it strictly. Within a few months, however, I had lost a great deal of weight and could no longer walk.

My parents and certainly my grandmother refused to accept the physician's prediction. They believed in and prayed for a healing. But when my condition worsened, my grandmother decided that if I was going to die, I was going to die full and happy. So she began to feed me all of my favorite foods—even the ones that were not on the diet.

After about eight months, I was still alive, though not much better or worse. But by the 12th month, I actually started to gain weight and to walk again. Around Easter, I walked outdoors for the first time in a year. That experience of taking in a fresh, beautiful spring day with all of my senses remains one of my brightest memories. Running in the wind, seeing the green of spring everywhere, inhaling the fragrances of flowers—I felt as if I had been born again. I thanked God then and I continue to thank God today for my survival.

When I finished high school, I wondered what I should do with this life that God had so graciously spared. My uncle, grandfather, and great-grandfather were all ministers, but in my early years that held no interest for me. Then, while in college, I became involved in the civil rights movement and began to see another side of the ministry. The Cleaver ministers had always dealt with the priestly components of ministry—serving their membership, teaching the Bible, preaching, and evangelizing. Then, with ministers like Martin Luther King and Ralph Abernathy involved in the civil rights movement, I understood how to minister to a world society.

Mixing the two—the priestly and the social action—held such a strong attraction for me that I could not resist becoming a part of it. As a minister and the mayor of a large midwestern city, I felt involved in a holistic practice of theology.

I'm glad I have persisted in following the calling to serve God and my fellow human beings. My mother, who started college while raising her children in public housing, taught us by word and by example that perseverance is a powerful tool in the human arsenal. Mother read *Daily Word* every single day—it was her daily support. There were two things my mother had to have every day when she got up in the morning: a strong cup of coffee and her *Daily Word*! When she came to visit Kansas City, she was awestruck by the fact that Unity Village, home of her beloved *Daily Word*, is nearby, and she was so excited to see the beauty of Unity Village with her own eyes.

The world God has given us is so full of beautiful and exciting places. Yet we don't need to be at a four-star hotel or in front of the Taj Mahal to experience the beauty of this world. Every person, place, and thing that God has created is special because the presence of God is there. God is with us whether we live in a shanty or a big house, in the country or in the city.

No matter where any of us are right now, we can experience a rebirth by knowing that God is with us. Through showing an appreciation for God and giving thanks for the life, the people, and the beauty that God has created, we truly experience the sweet mysteries of life.

Day 331

—◆—

Friends are those rare people who ask how we are
and then wait to hear the answer.
—Ed Cunningham

QUIET TALKS

Where do I go to receive answers to the questions on my mind or to discuss my innermost concerns? The answer lies within the quiet sanctuary of my soul, for there I commune with God.

As I speak, God listens. Without condemning me, God listens to my thoughts and concerns. I know that God is aware of all that I have experienced and understands how I feel, but being able to voice my thoughts fills me with an immediate sense of peace.

As I listen, God speaks to me. There is a sacred trust between God and me—a bond that can never be broken. As I listen to the guidance I receive from God, I relax and feel divine love assuring me of what I am to do. In my quiet talks with God, I experience the presence of God in every fiber of my being.

In my quiet talks with God, I discover true peace.

Day 332

♦

There comes that mysterious meeting in life when someone acknowledges who we are and what we can be, igniting the circuits of our highest potential.—Rusty Berkus

SHINE FORTH

Looking at the heavens on a starry night, I might imagine that God—in one sweeping motion—scattered the stars and planets so that each one fell into its perfect place. From a dark and seeming void of trillions of miles, the light of God's creativity sparkles brightly.

Making the truth of God's creativity personal to me, I realize that I can give to the Creator of all galaxies whatever concerns me. Out of this simple step of trusting God, I am relieved of worry and stress that cloud my vision and I am alert to the ways I can be a light of God in my world.

God created me to be a light of love and life. Letting go and letting God, I allow the light of God within me to shine forth in my life and out into my world.

I let go and let God's light shine forth.

Day 333

—◆—

*It is important to have a sense of partnership with God,
to understand you are not alone, to know that you
can be free in your prayers and honest about your needs.*
—Mary L. Kupferle

LIFE OF WHOLENESS

Do I believe that I can be healed? I do when I recognize that it is God's spirit within me that gives me life.

The life of God is a healing force that flows throughout my body. Every cell receives the healing energy of God—a light that bathes me in a warm glow that strengthens and renews me.

So if I need healing, I give thanks for God's healing life within me. I do not worry about what could go wrong or how or when I will be healed. Instead, I simply rest in God's presence and know with an unshakable faith that I am being healed.

I believe in the power of God within me, so I know that I can live a life of wholeness and strength.

**I believe that I am being healed
and made whole!**

Day 334

---◆---

*If someone listens, or stretches out a hand, or whispers
a word of encouragement, or attempts to understand
a lonely person, extraordinary things begin to happen.*
—*Loretta Girzartis*

QUALITY TIME Spending quality time with family and friends can be a beautiful experience—a special time of coming together and catching up with what has been happening in the lives of the ones I love most. Each moment is a time I will cherish, a time that nourishes my heart and strengthens my sense of closeness with others.

However, the time I spend with God is a feast for my soul, for God is the spiritual nourishment I long for and need in order to grow and flourish. Every thought of God renews me, and every moment spent in prayer builds a foundation that supports me and helps me to thrive. Each time I pray, my soul is satisfied by my awareness of God's spirit within me and God's love for me.

**I give God quality time, and God satisfies
every longing of my soul.**

Day 335

— ◆ —

The more we give of anything,
the more we shall get back.
—Grace Speare

FROM THE HEART   When I think someone has not been honest with me or has not been sincere about their own feelings, I may feel that a wonderful opportunity has been missed.

Yet how exhilarated I feel when I share a heart-and-soul connection with someone. Being with someone who is open to listening and to talking about what comes from deep within is a wonderful experience.

What joy I feel when I allow others to really know me and when I get to know them! I feel truly alive because I am more aware of God's spirit within me and all around me. I am in tune with the heartbeat of the universe. How refreshed I feel to be aware that I have touched the heart of God!

My words are inspired by God
and come from the heart.

DAILY WORD FOR FAMILIES

Day 336

—◆—

Behold the turtle. He only makes progress
when he sticks his neck out.
—James Bryant Conant

CREATED TO BE FREE

The spirit of God created me, and it is the life of God that lives in and through me. God created me to be free, to live a life of joy and love!

It's true: I am free with the freedom of Spirit! So I do not strive for the approval of others in order to be fulfilled in life. What is most important to me is to listen to God. When I follow through on the divine guidance I receive, I am doing what I feel in my soul is right to do.

I know that I can trust God's plan for me. In partnership with God, I act responsibly in charting my course through life. I have decisions to make daily; however, my first decision any day is to recognize my freedom of spirit.

My freedom is from God, and I honor this sacred gift by living a life of freedom now!

I am free with the freedom of Spirit,
living the life I was created to live.

Day 337

—◆—

*Just don't give up trying to do what you really want
to do. Where there's love and inspiration, I don't think
you can go wrong.—Ella Fitzgerald*

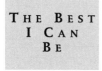 **THE BEST I CAN BE**

What does it mean to dedicate my life to God? It means that the actions I take and the choices I make convey the very character and nature of divine love.

I am dedicated to living a divinely directed life. From such a dedication, I find that I am never satisfied with doing less than my best because then I am being a blessing to others.

I act in loving ways and respond to others with understanding. As I do, I lay a foundation for living that will be a source of inspiration for the next generation to build upon.

I am dedicated to God and to being the best person I can be. Listening to divinely inspired ideas and following the guidance I receive, I fulfill my role in life.

**I am dedicated to God and to being
the best person I can be.**

Day 338

——◆——

Happiness is the sense
that one matters.
—Sarah Trimmer

UNQUENCHABLE JOY

When was the last time I saw or heard something that was so funny I could not contain my laughter? I feel happy in just remembering such a lighthearted moment!

Yet there is a deeper happiness, a joy of God, that is always within me. Joy bubbles up from within me to be a part of everything I do. The people I speak and interact with each day can hear joy in my voice and see joy on my face. With joy in my heart, I feel at ease. I know that I can meet any situation with a positive attitude.

Joy is a gladness of Spirit that lightens any burden and makes any task more enjoyable. God has given me the precious gift of joy, and I allow it to fill me to overflowing.

"Thank You, God, for the unquenchable joy of Your spirit that is living through me!"

Thank You, God, for the gift of joy!

Day 339

♦

Snowflakes are one of nature's most fragile things,
but just look what they can do when they stick together.
—Vista M. Kelly

PRESENCE OF PEACE The presence of God is everywhere. So each time I walk into my home, I want to remember that the presence of God is there to welcome me. I am living in a sacred atmosphere because the spirit of God permeates every room of my home.

My heart's desire is that the love of God be mirrored in the way I live with others in my home and how I treat visitors there. My home is a holy place, for the presence of God resides with me and my family and my friends.

The spirit of God within me and others in my home unites us so that love and understanding are conveyed in all our communication and interactions. God is a presence of peace, love, and understanding that allows my home to be a haven for me and my family and for all who enter its doors.

My home is filled with the sacred atmosphere
of God's presence.

Day 340

—◆—

Happiness is not having what you want,
but wanting what you have.
—Rabbi H. Schachtel

EXPERIENCE GRACE

Sweet, sweet Spirit, You fill my life with wonders! One I especially appreciate is the wonder of Your grace. Your love enfolds me and surrounds me wherever I may be.

Through Your unconditional love and acceptance, I experience the beauty of Your grace and realize that nothing can ever take Your love from me or diminish it in any way. The more I understand Your love for me, the more I want to be love in expression for the people in my life.

I am so grateful, God, for each experience that awakens in me a greater appreciation for You. I am beginning to understand that I, too, am a blessing—to You, to my family, and to the world!

God's love for me brings me a greater awareness of divine grace.

Day 341

The duty to be alive is the same as the duty to become oneself, to develop into the individual one potentially is.
—*Erich Fromm*

ACCEPTED AND LOVED My family is such an important part of who I am, yet a family is so much more than the people I call mother, father, sister, and brother.

Being part of a family makes me feel as if I am a part of something far greater than I could ever be on my own. It is knowing that I will be accepted and loved no matter how I look or sound.

I am an important member of God's universal family of love. So no matter where I might go, I am surrounded by the love and support of my global, spiritual family.

Being a member of God's universal family of love, I am comforted in knowing that I am always with people of kindred spirit.

I am a member of God's universal family of love.

Day 342

—◆—

If I really, actually leave all results quietly to God,
the instantaneous result is peace.
—Gardner Hunting

BLESSED WITH PEACE

At the innermost depths of my mind and heart, the spirit of God resides. The gentle touch of divine Spirit sweeps over my soul, assuring me that whatever I need, God is the fulfillment.

Every beat of my heart reminds me of God's love for me. As I allow my mind and body to relax in the sacred presence of God's unconditional love, I begin to feel peaceful and at rest.

Gently, quietly, God speaks to me, and I relax into the calm of love and peace that is permeating every cell of my body.

My trust in God is complete, for I know that, at the deepest level of my being, God and I are one. In that oneness, the love and peace that are my spiritual heritage will lead me in experiencing the wholeness of my life and my spirituality.

God blesses me with peace.

Day 343

———◆———

Never look down on anybody
unless you're helping him up.
—Jesse Jackson

BREATH OF LIFE   There are many kinds of healing needs. So as I pray for others, I remember to include people who are having health, relationship, or job-related challenges. In prayer I affirm life, love, and wisdom for them.

"God, I gain such peace of mind when I bring my loved ones to You in prayer. In this time of close communion with You, I know that Your healing presence is within me and within all those I include in prayer.

"Thank You, God, for the breath of life that first enlivened us, for the breath of life that continues to nourish us. Whatever my loved ones and I are going through, God, I know that You are with us. You are the life within that heals us, the love within that bonds us, and the wisdom within that guides us."

> I pray affirming life, love, and wisdom
> for my loved ones.

Day 344

—◆—

In the coldest February, as in every other month
in every other year, the best thing to hold on to
in this world is each other.—Linda Ellerbee

SACRED BOND One of the greatest blessings I can give another person is my love, which means that I hold that person in the highest regard.

I am united with others in a sacred bond of spiritual kinship. Whether or not I am related to someone by birth, I share a spiritual connection with that person. There is a sacred bond that unites people in relationships—as husband and wife, parent and child, co-workers, fellow students, and friends.

A sacred union of the soul is also a union of the mind and heart that enriches my life. Through my sacred soul connection with all humankind, I bring more love into the world—a love that is unconditional and that strengthens and supports us all the days of our lives.

I am united with others in a sacred bond
that is blessed by divine love.

DAILY WORD FOR FAMILIES

Day 345

—◆—

I believe that life is given us so that we may grow in love,
and I believe that God is in me as the sun is in the color
and fragrance of a flower.—Helen Keller

INVESTMENT OF FAITH God, it is remarkable, but the more I trust in You, the more I feel the powerful effects of my faith blessing me. In fact, the more I believe in You, the less stress and concern I experience. My faith in You is an investment that gives me more of what blesses me and less of what hinders me.

In those times when my faith seems to wane, Your grace moves in to support and encourage me. Because of Your unconditional love for me, You never ask how much faith I have; You only ask that I have faith.

So I declare what my faith tells me is always true: God, You are my constant companion. Your life moves throughout my body as energy. Your wisdom is the source of my understanding in all matters.

God, my faith in You blesses me.

Day 346

For the Children

Hello God,

I've noticed something about the kids in my school and at the park: Everybody looks and acts differently.

Even kids who are twins don't act the same. After I talk with them a while, I can tell them apart by the way they talk or the things they do.

All the faces I see look different. Tommy's nose is bigger than Billy's, and Suzy's hair is a different color than Amy's. Did You do this on purpose, God? I like it that way! We won't get bored because we won't know what the next person we meet will look like!

When I look in the mirror, I notice that my face is changing, too. It's growing along with my body! And what a great face it is! Thanks God, for making me the way I am.

Day 347

—◆—

*It is best to learn as we go, not go
as we have learned.
—Leslie Jeanne Sahler*

PRAYERFUL DECISIONS The day ahead of me is filled with choices—choices I will make for myself and for those who are in my care. Each choice will have an impact—sometimes major, sometimes minor—on how my day and my life are going.

Yet I do not worry about the decisions I make because I make them in cooperation with God. During my prayer times, God gives me the wisdom and guidance I need and points the way to my highest good.

I trust God and ask God to help me make my choices—from which foods to eat to what goals to set for myself and my family. With God, my choices are based on sound judgment and divine wisdom, so how can I ever go wrong?

**My choices are based on sound judgment
and inspired by divine guidance.**

Day 348

♦

The God who made the world and everything in it,
he who is Lord of heaven and earth . . . gives to all mortals
life and breath and all things.—Acts 17:24–25

CALMING THOUGHTS Whenever I feel confused or that my life is in disorder, I remember to always trust in God. I silently affirm to myself, "God, You are the shining light that guides me."

These simple words are a gentle reminder of what I know in my heart is true: God is always with me, enfolding me in love and assuring me that all is in divine order. Divine order is God's perfect plan for me.

Relying on God calms my thoughts. I feel secure because I know that God will lead me to the people and events that will contribute to my spiritual growth and fulfillment. All is in divine order because God is the order that supports and surrounds me.

God assures me that all is in divine order.

Day 349

---◆---

So many of our dreams at first seem impossible. And then they seem improbable. And then, when we summon the will, they soon become inevitable.—Christopher Reeve

NOW IS THE TIME! My childhood aspirations may not have become a reality in my life. Over time, what I considered to be important has changed as I have grown and matured. My faith in God has grown, too, prompting me to follow new dreams.

With faith in my heart, I face changes I had previously only thought about making, and I make them with the assurance that God is supporting me.

I accept the golden opportunities God has shown me and step forward with confidence. Now is the time for me to act on my faith and to experience the blessings God is offering me!

Now is the time for me to step forward in faith.

Day 350

♦

God writes the gospel not in the Bible alone,
but on trees and flowers and clouds and stars.
—Martin Luther

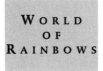

WORLD OF RAINBOWS A rainbow is made up of bands of different colors, yet it is the blending together of the differences within the rainbow that creates a beautiful, spectacular sight for all to see.

I live in a world of rainbows—a place of many different people. So I make a commitment to be an example of how one person can make a difference in the world by helping to create an atmosphere of love and harmony.

In this world, each person is essential to the whole and the whole supports each individual. Like the differences within the rainbow in the sky, the diversity of individuals in the world adds to the beauty and harmony of the whole world. Together we reflect harmony in a world of diversity for all to see and to follow.

As a prism of God's light, I reflect harmony to the world.

Day 351

—◆—

Treat your friends as you do your pictures,
and place them in their best light.
—Jennie Jerome Churchill

CONSTANT FORGIVENESS

If a burning match is placed in an airtight container, the fire will be extinguished. Without oxygen to feed the flame, the fire cannot last.

I know from my own experiences that when I forgive, I extinguish any angry thoughts within my mind so that I can be at peace.

Forgiveness moves me past replaying the events in my mind and working myself into a frenzy. Any spark of resentment or bitterness is quickly snuffed out by forgiveness.

As I picture each situation and each person surrounded by the love of God, I am able to release everything into God's care and keeping. With God as my constant inspiration, I forgive myself and others and live my life from the love and understanding within me.

> Because God is my inspiration,
> I forgive myself and others.

Day 352

—◆—

What we achieve inwardly
will change outer reality.
—Otto Rank

TRAVEL Sometimes, more than anything else, I want to retreat from all the busyness going on around me. Just being silent and still for a few moments—thinking of nothing else but the presence of God—refreshes me.

Then I am ready to go on with the day, with my plans, with my life. When my day and my plans include travel, I let my ongoing awareness of God continue to refresh me. Moving through traffic on a street or highway, rushing to make connections at an airport or a bus stop, I remain calm and alert.

The spirit of God is with me wherever I am and accompanies me wherever I travel. In my own neighborhood or in some faraway place, I am enfolded in the holy presence of God. I am safe and secure.

Wherever I am, wherever I travel, I am enfolded
in the presence of God.

Day 353

—◆—

If I could wish for my life to be perfect, it would be tempting; but I would have to decline, for life would no longer teach me anything.—Allyson Jones

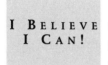

I BELIEVE I CAN! At a time of challenge or opportunity, I am given a boost past my own thoughts of limitation when someone says to me, "I believe you can do it!"

That person is right, for I will get past the challenge and on to the achievement. Yet how can another person know more about me than I know about myself? It must be that the one who encourages me knows I have potential because the presence of God is within me.

This is the truth I need to recognize for myself at all times, and I need to know this truth for others as well. With an encouraging word, someone else can confirm what is true: "You can accomplish amazing things, because God within you is your wisdom, your strength, and your creativity."

My answer is this: "Yes, I believe I can!"

God within me is my wisdom, my strength, and my creativity.

Day 354

—◆—

To love and be loved is to feel
the sun from both sides.
—David Viscott

COMFORTING WORDS

I want to comfort friends and loved ones who turn to me in a time of need or crisis, and I know I can when I rely on the inspiration of God. The right words to express and the actions to take will come to me and from me because God is guiding me.

In a sacred atmosphere of prayer, I am comforted. From my own experience with God, I learn how to comfort my loved ones. God loves everyone and expresses love through all who are willing.

I share the truth of God's love and our unlimited ability to love with my family and friends. Being a good listener is important, and I speak from the heart to let people know that I do care. I can comfort others in their time of need, for the God of love guides me in giving love and assurance to others.

I give the comfort of love and assurance to others.

Day 355

—◆—

My soul is awakened,
my spirit is soaring.
—Anne Brontë

WHISPER OF HOPE

When my courage and energy seem to be in short supply, this is the time I need to be sensitive to the gentlest of sounds and thoughts and feelings.

The balmy breeze, not the howling wind, refreshes me. The peaceful thoughts I think are the ones that calm me and allow me to function best. The soft voice of encouragement I hear is God's message of hope being whispered to me. That whisper has the power of the Almighty behind it.

Out of those tender thoughts, feelings, sounds, and messages, I gain new purpose in living. I am the gentle person I truly desire to be. God is gentle with me, and I am gentle with myself and others. It is the power of the Almighty that I hear, touch, and feel as gentleness in my daily life.

God whispers a message of hope to me.

Day 356

—◆—

First keep peace within yourself,
then you can also bring peace to others.
—Thomas à Kempis

UNITED IN SPIRIT

Today, I may be getting together with family and friends to share good times and good food. What a blessing such sharing will be for us all.

Yet if we are separated by many miles or I am unable to be with my loved ones, I give thanks that I am united with them in spirit. I can always be close to them in my thoughts and prayers:

"Thank You, God, for the gift of family and friends—for the blessing of loved ones who share my life and for the love I receive from them.

"Knowing that Your loving presence will forever grace me and my loved ones is the greatest gift I could ask for myself or for them. Whether we are near or far, we are forever united by Your spirit within us. Thank You, God, for all of our blessings!"

Thank You, God, for all of our blessings.

Day 357

---◆---

It is difficult to steer a parked car,
so get moving.
—Henrietta Mears

I FOLLOW GOD

New electronic equipment and appliances come with an instruction manual as a guide to learning all that new technologies are capable of doing. At times I may wonder if life would be simpler if I had an instruction manual to learn all I am capable of doing and being. Yet when I think about it, I realize I have something better: God is an unlimited source of information that I can turn to anytime.

If I am feeling uncertain about my abilities—whether I am starting a new job or beginning a new project—God assures me that I am a capable person. I am blessed with divinely inspired ideas and filled with the confidence to forge ahead. Wherever God guides me, I will follow.

> **I follow God's guidance with faith in God**
> **and with confidence in my abilities.**

Day 358

—◆—

*When there is only one race
and that's mankind, we shall be free.*
—*Garth Brooks*

UNIQUE Walking beside a creek of gently flowing water, I may see hundreds of stones that look alike. Yet when I look at individual stones, I see a great variety of sizes, shapes, colors, and textures. Each stone is unique.

I may have tended to view people as alike, too. Only after appreciating the uniqueness of the individuals in the world did I see the incredible variety, texture, and shape of God's creativity.

We are each unique. Living and working together, we bring the blessings of our talents and abilities, our goals and dreams to each new day and to one another. There is no lack among us. The uniqueness of each individual contributes something of value to the whole as we let the spirit of God within live through us.

**I am a beloved creation of God, sharing
a spiritual kinship with everyone.**

DAILY WORD FOR FAMILIES

Day 359

—◆—

True wisdom lies in gathering the precious things
out of each day as it goes by.
—E. S. Bouton

CHERISH GOD

The wonder of God is all around me! It is in the wind that caresses my face and saturates the very air I breathe. As I watch children at play and listen to their laughter, I marvel at the wonder God has created.

There is so much to give thanks for in a world of God's creation, and so I feel a true sense of thanksgiving every day. Every day I live my life in celebration of the wonder of God by expressing the joy and peace I feel in my heart.

I cherish the beautiful planet that is home to me and to all that God has created. As the sun warms my face or a bird sings to me, I experience the wonder of God's presence. Today and every day is a celebration of the glory of God.

I cherish each day as a celebration
of the wonder of God.

Day 360

—◆—

Truly loving another means letting go of all expectations. It means full acceptance, even celebration, of another's personhood.—Karen Casey

SUNSHINE OF LOVE

When I give thanks for all that enriches me, I include every opportunity to be a blessing: "God, I feel Your love flowing out from me when I am kind and compassionate. Each loving word or deed by me enriches my life with the joy of giving. With every blessing I give, I am blessed in return."

I appreciate the people who bring the sunshine of love and acceptance into my life—every day and when especially needed: "God, I am thankful for the people who bless me. The understanding, friendship, and love they share light up my life. I feel so good knowing that I am loved and appreciated."

Being aware of my prosperity, I realize that God is the source of each blessing, of each person blessing me, and of each opportunity for me to be a blessing: "God, thank You for loving me and for enriching me. Thank You, God, for everything!"

God is the source of all that enriches my life.

Day 361

—◆—

Drink it all in . . . there is no way to happiness;
happiness IS the way.
—Wayne W. Dyer

TRUE IDENTITY

God, I may have spent so much of my time wondering about my purpose in life as a human being that I have overlooked my true identity as a spiritual being.

That was in the past. Now, dear God, since I have experienced an awakening to Your spirit within me, I know that my purpose is to be an expression of Your love, life, and wisdom.

What is so amazing is this: I have awakened not only to Your presence within me, but also to Your presence within everyone, within all places and situations.

The more aware I am spiritually, the more alive I feel physically. I am whole and holy. What a relief it is to know that You are always with me. You have welcomed me home to Your kingdom, where peace and love flow through me as a divine inheritance from You.

I am awake to and remain aware of my true identity as a spiritual being.

Day 362

—◆—

Stop a moment, cease your work,
and look around you.
—Thomas Carlyle

A L W A Y S
R E M E M B E R

In a stress-filled moment, I may say something that is a quick reaction which hurts another person's feelings. Afterward, however, simple words such as "I'm sorry" or "Let's talk" can be the hardest to say.

Yet what seems so hard on my own becomes easy when I remember to ask God to help me. I contribute harmony and understanding that go a long way in promoting goodwill toward others.

I nurture harmonious feelings by doing my best not to react in anger but to respond with love. I think before I speak and always remember God's golden rule of treating others as I want to be treated, which is with love and compassion.

All people are God's people, and I give to others the love and respect that every child of God is worthy of receiving.

I always remember to promote
harmony wherever I am.

Day 363

We have this hope, a sure
and steadfast anchor of the soul.
—Hebrews 6:19

**A LIFE
OF FAITH**

There are signs and wonders of God's presence all around me. Some may not be so obvious as to amaze me, but I can still recognize them for what they are. I can because my belief in God opens my eyes to the glory of God in even the ordinary things in life. Then I know without a doubt that God is taking care of me.

If I am troubled, a song being played on the radio can serve as a soothing balm on my emotions. If questions linger in my mind, the next person I meet may say something in conversation that is the perfect answer or causes me to recognize that I already know what the answer is.

Through a belief in and an awareness of God, I am guided in living a life of faith—a life in which I am greatly blessed.

The presence of God surrounds me.

Day 364

—◆—

It is never too late to be
what you might have been.
—*George Eliot*

NEW DAWN

There is a new dawn breaking for me today, for this is a day in which hope and faith, courage and determination are reborn in me.

I feel that rebirth as peace rising within me, because God's spirit is giving me understanding about both the challenges and opportunities that are before me.

With the dawn of the new day, God shows me that what may have looked like a mountain only yesterday is in reality a small hill I can climb. So I move forward in a life of learning and accomplishment.

This is a new day, and I am reborn. I experience a spiritual rebirth in which I am renewed both emotionally and physically. I thank God that thought by thought, cell by cell, I am healed and renewed!

The light of spiritual understanding shines brightly within me today.

Day 365

---◆---

Circle of Love

A wedding ring is symbolic of the love and commitment a couple share: There is no beginning or end to the ring, for it has been forged into an eternal circle that signifies the couple's future together.

All of our relationships—as couples, families, friends, and co-workers—are entwined in a never-ending circle—the circle of love that is shared by all of God's creations. We recognize the sacredness of one another.

Each of us has a responsibility to carry love within our hearts wherever we may go. This love is a divine blessing from God—the Creator and Sustainer of all life.

We have come full circle—there is no longer a beginning or an ending, for we are one with the eternal, everlasting spirit of God. Where once there may have been a sense of separation, there now is a unity of love and caring.

The most beautiful action in the world is to love.
The second most beautiful is to give.
—Bertha von Suttner

ABOUT THE
FEATURED AUTHORS

June Allyson is a multi-faceted actress, singer, and dancer on stage, screen, and television. Her career has included 23 films and many appearances on television, including her own show, *The DuPont Show With June Allyson*. June is actively involved in charity work for the June Allyson Foundation and works as an advocate for senior issues.

Bob Barker, host of television's *The Price Is Right*, has received 12 Emmys and the Carbon Mike Award of the Pioneer Broadcasters. He established the DJ & T Foundation, named in memory of his wife, Dorothy Jo, and his mother, Tilly, to support low-cost or free spay/neuter clinics. Bob's work on behalf of animals has garnered him a long list of awards from humane organizations across the country.

Emanuel Cleaver is a former mayor of Kansas City, Missouri, and serves as pastor of St. James United Methodist Church. He has received numerous awards, including the All-America City Award and the Governor's Award for "Local Elected Official of the Year." Mayor Cleaver and his wife, Dianne, have four children.

Richard Jafolla, former director of Silent Unity, is an ordained Unity minister. He is co-author with his wife, Mary-Alice, of *Nourishing the Life Force, The Quest, Adventures on the Quest, Quest '96, Quest '97,* and *Quest 2000*. Richard is also the co-author of numerous pamphlets, national magazine articles, and several cassette tapes.

Naomi Judd and her daughter Wynonna received six Grammys and a number of other awards and honors during their eight years together as a country-music duo. Naomi is highly sought after as an inspirational speaker, and her books include the best-seller *Love Can Build a Bridge* and *Naomi's Home Companion: A Treasury of Favorite Recipes, Food for Thought, and Kitchen Wit and Wisdom.*

Bil Keane is the creator of the internationally syndicated cartoon "The Family Circus," which appears in 1,500 newspapers and is read by 100 million people daily. Bil became president of the National Cartoonist Society in 1981, and he has won many awards, including the prestigious Reuben Award.

Richard Maraj, an ordained Unity minister, is a renowned speaker and workshop presenter. He is a member of the National Speakers Association and speaks for corporations, government agencies, churches, and charitable organizations.

Elaine Meyer has been the assistant editor of *Daily Word* magazine since 1992. She is also co-author and co-editor of *Daily Word: Love, Inspiration, and Guidance for Everyone, Daily Word Prayer Journal,* and *Daily Word for Women.*

Lynda Wells is a performance coach and musical-theater instructor at the Singers Forum, a nonprofit vocal arts center in New York City. She is a published writer and the personal manager of her dear friend, actress June Allyson. Prior to her career behind the scenes, Lynda was a successful television commercial actress, with over 150 national commercials to her credit.

Maurice Williams, an ordained Unity minister, served for 7 years as an instructor at Unity School for Religious Studies in

ABOUT THE FEATURED AUTHORS

Unity Village, Missouri. He traveled extensively throughout the United States and abroad, speaking and presenting healing workshops.

Janie Wright has been associate editor of *Daily Word* magazine since 1989. She is also co-author and co-editor of *Daily Word: Love, Inspiration, and Guidance for Everyone*, *Daily Word Prayer Journal*, and *Daily Word for Women*.

Colleen Zuck has been editor of *Daily Word* magazine since 1985. She also served as editor of *Wee Wisdom*, the longest continually published magazine for children in the United States. She is co-author and co-editor of *Daily Word: Love, Inspiration, and Guidance for Everyone*; *Daily Word Prayer Journal*; and *Daily Word for Women*.

About the Featured Authors